LITERARY CRITICISM AND CULTURAL THEORY

THE INTERACTION OF TEXT AND SOCIETY

edited by

WILLIAM E. CAIN
WELLESLEY COLLEGE

A COINCIDENCE OF WANTS

THE NOVEL AND NEOCLASSICAL ECONOMICS

CHARLES R. LEWIS

Routledge
Taylor & Francis Group
New York London

First published 2000 by Garland Publishing, Inc.

This edition published 2013 by Routledge
711 Third Avenue, New York, NY 10017
2 Park Square, Milton Park, Abingdon, Oxon OX14 4RN

Routledge is an imprint of the Taylor & Francis Group, an informa business

A version of Chapter 5 has previously appeared in "Desire and Indifference in *Sister Carrie:* Neoclassical Economic Anticipations." *Dreiser Studies,* Vol. 29, No. 1–2 (1998), 18–33.

Library of Congress Cataloging-in-Publication Data

Lewis, Charles R., 1959-
A coincidence of wants : the novel and neoclassical economics / Charles R. Lewis
p. cm.— (Literary criticism and cultural theory)
Includes bibligraphical references and index.
ISBN 0-8153-3648-9 (alk. paper)
1. Neoclassical school of economics. 2. Literature — History and criticism. I. Title. II. Series

HB98.2 .L48 1999
330.15'7—dc21 99-052038

for Maisie, Avery, and Nora

Contents

Preface

My title, *A Coincidence of Wants: The Novel and Neoclassical Economics*, makes reference to a scenario that economists use to describe a necessary condition for exchange. Direct barter is possible between two parties when each one wants what the other possesses. They must also agree on the terms of exchange between them and be able to effect the transaction on those terms. When this coincidence of wants is absent or goes unrecognized, a medium of exchange is necessary to realize the coincidence and effect the transaction, which is of course one of the functions of money.

These two economic scenarios of exchange, involving the presence of a coincidence and the need to produce one, together resemble the predicament of the literary critic seeking to bring about some sort of transaction between the novel and political economy. Perhaps this is especially true in contemporary interdisciplinary approaches to literary study. For while the function of literary criticism is often described in terms analogous to the other two functions of money (as a measure and store of value), poststructuralist criticism and theory often takes as its task the realization of a variety of possible exchanges between literary and nonliterary discourse, as well as between their respective textual economies and the cultural and historical conditions of their production and reception.

My use of the term "coincidence of wants" is intended to denote a number of coincidences involving the novel and the mainstream tradition of neoclassical economic analysis. Previous economic readings of specific novels or of the genre more widely rarely make reference to neoclassical perspectives, which have held a key position in the formal analysis of the marketplace for over a century. By underscoring how a neoclassical framework variously complements and challenges other economic interpretations of four novels, I hope to enrich our understanding of the literal and symbolic economies in novelistic fiction. In Chapter 1, I survey key aspects of neoclassical economic analysis and its relation to classical and Marxist economics, discuss examples of literary criticism and theories of the novel that are especially relevant to my own approach, and offer a short description of each of my four arguments. The chapters that follow address narrative and capital formation in Daniel Defoe's *Robinson Crusoe;* individual enterprise in Mary Shelley's *Frankenstein*; the monetized romance of international trade in Herman Melville's *Moby Dick*; and consumer desire and indifference in Theodore Dreiser's *Sister Carrie.*

While working on this material, I spent several years walking back and forth on the Washington Avenue Bridge, which spans the Mississippi River and links what are called the West and East Banks at the University of Minnesota. English sits on one side and Economics lies on the other, and I came to find in that geography yet another metaphor for my interdisciplinary work, sometimes focusing on the water, sometimes on the bridge. So, while speaking of bridges, I should acknowledge Kent Bales, Marty Roth, Chester Anderson, and John Mowitt in the Department of English, as well as John Chipman from the Department of Economics, all of whom helped me span two very different plots of ground in writing the dissertation that ultimately evolved into this book. And I am grateful to my colleagues at Westminster College, who in addition to many other kindnesses, supported the final stage with a research grant. Finally, my thanks to friends and family, especially Shawn Gillen, Tom Reynolds, David Pink, Charlie Sugnet, and Bob Solotaroff, and most of all to my wife Julie, who has always helped me manage the currents to be crossed.

I intend the four novels and handful of neoclassical concepts brought together here to suggest something much more like a set of case studies than a determined theory of literary genre or a sweeping interdisciplinary history. Perhaps that is the task of another work. In the meanwhile, I hope that the coincidence of wants bid for here is itself an exchange that both satisfies now and points to the possibilities of future returns.

Charles R. Lewis
Westminster College
Fulton, Missouri

A COINCIDENCE OF WANTS

CHAPTER 1

Wading into Foucault's Paddling Pool

Near the beginning of *Wealth of Nations*, Adam Smith proposes a provocative connection between economic and linguistic exchange. He argues that the division of labor—for Smith the cornerstone of economic progress—"is not originally the effect of any human wisdom, which foresees and intends that general opulence to which it gives occasion" (25). Instead, economic specialization and exchange are

> the necessary, though very slow and gradual consequence of a certain propensity in human nature . . . to truck, barter, and exchange one thing for another. Whether this propensity be one of those original principles in human nature, of which no further account can be given; or whether, as seems more probable, it be the necessary consequence of the faculties of reason and speech, it belongs not to our present subject to enquire. (25)

Smith makes this point more directly in *Lectures on Jurisprudence*, where, referring to the division of labor, he argues, "The real foundation of it is that principle to persuade which so much prevails in human nature" (493). Capitalism, according to this originary text of modern political economy, emerges in part as an unintended material effect of rhetoric.

Smith also suggests that economic progress, in turn, brings with it specialization and advance in the production of prose. In *Lectures on Rhetoric and Belles Lettres*, he argues:

> Thus it is that Poetry is cultivated in the most Rude and Barbarous nations, often to a considerable perfection; whereas they make no attempt towards the improvement of Prose. Tis the Introduction of Commerce, or at least of the opulence that is commonly the attendant of Commerce which first brings on the improvement of Prose. (137)

Smith also observes that "[p]rose is the Stile in which all the common affairs of Life, all Business and Agreements are made. No one ever made a Bargain in verse; pleasure is not what he there aims at."

However problematic we might find this account of historical change, cultural difference, and the form and function of human expression, Smith's claim about economic activity and its relation to prose resonates with three familiar observations in literary studies of the novel: its use of prose as its mode of expression, its tendency to take the "common affairs of life" as its subject matter, and its depiction of that subject matter in narratives in which characters and conditions undergo a developmental change or progress. Indeed, a long tradition in studies of the novel has argued for a variety of important connections between this literary genre and the conditions and discourses of capitalism.[1] Novels offer representations of subjectivity, models of agency, determinations of value, and resolutions of both individual and societal desires in view of their respective and interrelated obstacles. Political economy can be said to do much of the same. Given Smith's remarks, as well as the eighteenth-century coincidence between the emergence of modern economic analysis and the rise of the novel, we should not be surprised at the likelihood of extensive "truck, barter, and exchange" between these two areas of prose whose progress traces a number of shared historical and cultural ties to market capitalism over the last three centuries.

Studies of the novel and its relation to market capitalism take a variety of approaches. Some focus on the fictional mimetic representation of capitalism (Pip's upwardly mobile "expectations"). Others have gone another step and argued that formal technical aspects of fiction can be linked to market conditions (Pip's narrative point of view as a performance of economic alienation). Others have given more attention to the material conditions of book publishing itself (Pip serialized). Still others have "reversed the charges" and proposed that these capitalist conditions and discourses are themselves reciprocally affected by the circulation of novels in the social imagination (Pip's "cultural work"). Broadly speaking, studies of the novel addressing capitalist representation and reality tend to fall into one or more of the following categories: First, a focus on the historical conditions of capitalism, such as urbanization, industrialization, and mass-production and consumption; Second, an emphasis on texts and discourses (other than formal economic analysis) with important ties to market capitalism, such as law, journalism, and advertising; And finally, a discussion of formal economic analysis that is confined to classical and/or Marxist economics. Little attention, however, has been given by literary critics to the neoclassical economic analysis that emerged toward the end of the nineteenth century and is still of profound importance in the way the market economy is represented by both economists and non-economists alike. Despite Michel Foucault's claim in *The Order of Things* that differences between "bourgeois" and "revolutionary" economics amount to "no more than storms in a children's paddling pool" (262), the indifference of literary critics toward the neoclassical mainstream tradition has resulted in a significant oversight in the criticism and theory of the novel, especially (although not exclusively) in regard to those studies that would read the novel in relation to political economy. This study proposes that neoclassical analysis—along with its relation to other economic perspectives and literary study of the novel—is indeed a paddling pool worth wading into.

A number of other preliminary comments need to be made about assumptions, scope, and objectives. The first point involves the question of the assumed reader, a clarification that is perhaps especially necessary in an interdisciplinary project of this sort. Although this study is directed primarily toward literary critics interested in the novel, I make fairly extensive use of a select number of issues in neoclassical economic analysis. I assume that the reader either will be generally unfamiliar with neoclassical analysis, or will know of it but reject it as an economic model, or will have not found it useful as an interpretive point of reference for reading novelistic fiction. My use of neoclassical theory attempts to address only the first and third possibilities, while avoiding the second, as this study is not intended to be a defense of, or a challenge to, some essential claim about neoclassical theory as a representation of economic reality. If it can be shown that its economic concepts can be deployed to produce useful readings of particular novels, as well as to produce interesting connections between economic and literary discourse more broadly, it will be left to the reader to decide about the use-value or exchange-value of neoclassical theory.

A second point involves the identity and scope of the twined objects of this study, the novel and mainstream economic theory. The novel is, of course, a problematic genre to define, just as its instantiations can be difficult to delineate. The novel is indeed a genre that Henry James usefully referred to as the "baggy monster," one of whose identifying traits, as theorists such as Georg Lukács and M. M. Bakhtin have argued, is precisely its formal and historical plasticities. The convenient description of a "fictional prose narrative of an extended length" is a beginning point that, while delivering us to no end of distinctions, exceptions, and approximations, nevertheless allows us to recount some of its more familiarly listed attributes: the use of common speech forms, the representation of relatively recognizable and probable personal experience and social conditions, a treatment of surface sensory detail, a focus on the subjective and objective states of characters whose development is both fictionally imagined and formally rendered in an extended written prose narration of events, and a formal and thematic propensity for broadly ironic configurations.[2] One might, of course, take exception to each of these characteristics by finding novelistic examples that trouble such "defining" descriptors, just as those traits could be found in other sorts of written texts and modes of expression both within and beyond the historical and cultural frameworks in which the novel is conventionally located. The point is happily admitted rather than rigorously engaged.

Indeed, this speaks somewhat to my point regarding the coincidence between the novel and modern political economy. For example, critical descriptions of novelistic irony resemble classical representations of economic scarcity. This coincidence involves not just a version of a predicament, but also the structural dynamics of those formal discursive systems in which that predicament is played out. In *The Theory of the Novel*, for instance, Georg Lukács makes a distinction between the ancient "integrated" civilizations that produced the "organic" fixities of the epic and the more "problematic" conditions of modernity represented in the form and content of the novel. Lukács' distinction suggests a link between the historical development of capitalism, with its emphasis on individualism, social mobility, and economic change, and the novelistic depiction of the "problematic individual" (78) whose "transcendental homelessness" (41) is a fundamentally ironic predicament marked by a constant state of "becoming" (73). M. M. Bakhtin pursues a similar distinction between the epic and the novel, in which he argues for three distinguishing characteristics of the latter: its linguistic diversity or "polyglossia," its "temporal coordinates" linking past and present, and the "open-endedness" of form afforded by this "zone of maximal contact with the present" (11-2). Like Lukács, Bakhtin speaks of the "man [who has] ceased to coincide with himself" (35) and the "incongruity of a man with himself" whose surplus of "unrealized potential and unrealized demands" constitutes an ironic predicament created by "the zone of contact with an inconclusive present" (37) that is always a "developing reality" (39).

Like Lukács' and Bakhtin's descriptions of novelistic irony, classical and neoclassical representations of the condition of *homo economicus* present us with a fundamentally ironic mode of storytelling, with its organizing claim of an unbridgeable gap between wants and resources—a ratio whose name is scarcity. This scarcity, in turn, forces individuals and societies to allocate their limited resources efficiently and equitably, which is best realized by market mechanisms. These mechanisms constitute a protean system of constant change that, like Bakhtin's description of the novel, "is plasticity itself. . . . a genre that structures itself in a zone of direct contact with developing reality" (39). Market economists describe a market that is always both changing (due to the unfulfilled striving of self-interested individuals) and tending toward equilibrium (due to responsive adjustment mechanisms in the market), which is not unlike Lukács' depiction of the novel, with its "unfillable, sentimental striving . . . [that] is balanced and brought to rest" (77), even as this equilibrium is constantly changing: "The composition of the novel is the paradoxical fusion of heterogeneous and discrete components into an organic whole which is then abolished over and over again" (84). This critical poetics of novelistic irony resembles a market poetics of economic scarcity.

Perhaps this is an excessively formal analogy or an all-too-easy bet on a pair of cards drawn from the hand of modernity. Yet it speaks to the point that those characteristics associated with the novel can only ever be partly accurate, just as they will also be accurate in other parts. That said, the selection of the novels (*Robinson Crusoe*, *Frankenstein*, *Moby Dick*, and *Sister Carrie*) is intended to reflect some breadth of the Anglo-American tradition (two English and two American), chronological scope (almost two hundred years), and periodic and stylistic range (from romance to naturalism). They are not intended to suggest comprehensiveness within the historical and formal boundaries of the novel or to argue for the exclusivity of the novel as a literary site of economic configuration. Instead, they are meant to serve as relatively diverse (if largely canonical) case studies of the discursive affinities between two specific sites of literary and economic representation within the shared historical and social framework of modern capitalism.

The question of definitions and boundaries of literary genre raises a similar problem regarding the designation of neoclassical economics.

Neoclassical economic theory marks an important shift in the mainstream tradition that emerged in England, Europe, and America late in the nineteenth century and continues to have a strong impact on how the market economy is formally studied and popularly represented today. Without getting ahead of the story (I survey key aspects of economic theory below), neoclassical analysis shares closes ties to its classical antecedents, while also presenting a number of important differences. Likewise, classical theory, while conventionally seen as marking the advent of modern political economy sometime in the eighteenth century, shares many links with its antecedents, such as mercantilist and physiocratic thought. My assumption is that while the eighteenth century is indeed an appropriate and productive place to observe important developments in modern economic discourse, the emergence of the neoclassical elaboration of classical analysis a century later helps to amplify the affinities and affiliations among market analysis, novelistic fiction, and its literary study.

The term "neoclassical" necessarily suggests a link with a classical antecedent, and this link has long been a question for economists: in what ways are classical and neoclassical analysis the same, and how are they different? They are typically represented as a part of the same mainstream tradition of market analysis, yet one can find in the literature substantial disagreement about whether the neoclassical period represents a turning away from, or an elaboration of, the classical period. This question bears upon my own project, insofar as economic concepts that appear in both classical and neoclassical analysis are deployed in my readings of the novels. At some points, differences, shifts, and discrepancies are emphasized, whereas in other areas similarities and consistencies are more crucial. While the term "neoclassical" can sometimes refer to the entire mainstream tradition that encompasses both the classical and neoclassical phases, the distinction between them will be underscored throughout this study.

II. THE CLASSICAL TRADITION AND NEOCLASSICAL ELABORATIONS

A more extensive inventory of some key points of mainstream classical and neoclassical analysis helps to stake out this economic landscape, as well as provide a backdrop for a closer look in the next section at other critical interpretations of the novel that make use of economic concepts. For while many literary critics have at least some passing familiarity with classical and Marxist theory, apparently relatively fewer of them are aware of, or interested in, neoclassical analysis. It should also be noted that this overview is in part intended to bring into relief those economic concerns that are most relevant to the readings of the four novels given in this study. These topics include capital formation and economic growth, the identity and function of the entrepreneur, the nominal and real effects of money, and the utility theory of consumption.

As already noted, the beginning of classical political economy is as problematic as that of the novel. Indeed, this problem is nicely brought together in the economic and literary works of Daniel Defoe, for just as Defoe's *Robinson Crusoe* is challenged as the "first novel" as often as it is cited as such, so too have literary critics and economists alike debated Defoe's place in the history of economic thought, as his writings reflect both pre-classical mercantilist and classical free-trade sensibilities.[3] Similarly, Adam Smith's *Wealth of Nations* (published almost sixty years after *Robinson Crusoe*) is a conventional starting point of the classical tradition, although this, too, is something of an originary fiction; one can find many important pre-classical anticipations of Smith's work, as well as argue that physiocratic, mercantilist and classical discourse all have more in common than is sometimes recognized. Moreover, economic historians such as Joseph Schumpeter claim that Smith was as much of a timely synthesizer and popularizer as he was an innovative economic thinker.[4] Nevertheless, Smith's work was a profoundly important articulation of classical thought in his own time and it has remained so ever since, and it is therefore a useful reference for surveying some key classical concerns and concepts.

In the most general terms, Smith's classical analysis deploys eighteenth-century Newtonian concepts of natural law to propose both the possibility and the desirability of a self-regulating market economy comprised of self-interested individuals. Smith's work addresses the source and distribution of wealth, capital accumulation and economic growth, and the role of government in the economy. These concerns are reflected in the organization and content of the five books of Smith's *Wealth of Nations*. Book I addresses the "Causes of Improvement in the productive Powers of Labour, and of the Order according to which its Produce is naturally distributed among the different Ranks" (3). Here Smith makes the division of labor the cornerstone of economic productivity and growth. Smith describes a distribution of wealth by way of allocative pricing mechanisms that register both the contributions of and returns to the owners of the factors of production (land, labor, and capital). However, if the market price (and the real value) of an economic good is determined and signified by the cost of production, what is the role of demand in determining price and value? For in some way, producer supply *and* consumer demand—both the sweat of the brow and the glint in the eye, as it were—play a role in market outcomes. This is one area of Smith's analysis that has been the object of much debate ever since: Is labor the source or measure of value? Is labor the only source of value, or do other production factors make distinct and irreducible contributions? If value is created by the costs embodied in production (whether only labor or otherwise), how is the value of a commodity linked to a market price in which demand plays a role? In one sense, this first book contains many of the problems related to the theory of value—its sources and significations—that delineate the various directions in which economic analysis has gone ever since. One of the key points to note here is that while classical economists discussed value in terms of production costs (especially the Ricardians) and the interaction between supply and demand (Malthus, Senior, and Mill), the neoclassical analysts significantly reformulated these questions by focusing on demand, where the problem of value is revised into a question of consumer utility.

Book II of *Wealth of Nations* addresses the "Nature, Accumulation, and Employment of Stock" (4). Here Smith explores the means by which economies grow, the primary instrument being capital. This is a key section for Smith's famous claims regarding the importance of "parsimony" for growth, for the ability to accumulate capital and realize economic growth is, for Smith, closely tied to the ability and willingness to defer and detour the consumption of economic resources into more productive configurations. Again, Smith raises many critical questions that have been explored by economists ever since: How do we define capital? What are the differences between capital and consumer goods? How do productivity and durability figure in this distinction? What is the relationship between capital and the other factors of production? What are the returns that accrue to capital? And how do capital accumulation and economic growth structure and sustain one another? One important point to note is that with the neoclassical elaboration of capital theory (such as Böhm-Bawerk's), Smith's notion of "parsimony" (or Senior's "abstinence") is increasingly articulated in terms of an economic agent (whether individual, firm, or nation) who faces a trade-off between present and future consumption, who cannot simply defer consumption but must actively detour economic capacities into "roundabout" productive configurations, and who realizes their returns as a temporal sequentiation of a material difference. While much of this can be found in or inferred from classical analysis, neoclassical theory sketches in a solitary Crusoe-like figure whose isolated and abstracted microeconomic predicament brings this capital narrative of delay, detour, and return into full relief.

Book III of *Wealth of Nations*, in addressing the "different Progress of Opulence in different Nations," asks what conditions and choices involving capital must be realized for economic growth to occur, and how different national histories reflect this. This short section is something of a prelude to Book IV, in which Smith turns to that subject for which he is perhaps most recognized, his free-trade challenge to mercantilist trade regulation and protection. Much of the mercantilist position related to arguments about maintaining a positive balance of trade, as well as maximizing the domestic money supply of gold, which was seen as the key to national wealth. Classical economists generally argued that real national wealth would increase if market forces were left free to play themselves out, hence the doctrine of "laissez-faire" that would let the "invisible hand" efficiently and equitably generate economic growth. Any artificial controls or mercantilist protections such as collusive monopolies (including colonialist protections) create "derangements" (to use Smith's term) in the efficiency of the "natural" mechanisms of the system. (At the same time, it is useful to remember that in Book V Smith turns to that topic for which he is perhaps least known, his discussion of the role of government, with its functions of defense, justice, public works, and the facilitation of commerce.)

One important collateral question involves this relationship between the creation of "real" wealth and the role of money—whether money essentially plays a neutral role as a nominal signifier of real conditions, or somehow makes a real difference in those conditions. The quantity theory of money, for example, established a relation between money supply and price levels, but the question remained as to whether changes in the quantity of money and prices had a material impact on employment, output, and distribution. This debate, however, cannot quite be framed as a distinction between non-neutral mercantilists (who emphasized the real role of money in the stimulation of trade) and the neutral free-traders (who tended to focus on other "real" sources of wealth), for this long-standing question of the relation between monetary representation and economic reality is debated within mercantilist, classical, and neoclassical analyses.

As with classical theory, determining the origins of neoclassical analysis is problematic. Classical political economy, as represented in most economic textbooks and histories of economic thought, generally refers to that period of mainstream market analysis that begins with Smith's *Wealth of Nations* (1776) and continues at least until the publication of John Stuart Mill's *Principles of Political Economy* in 1848, although sometimes Mill's death in 1873 serves as a designation of the end of the classical period, since this was the decade in which emerged the neoclassical changes introduced by Carl Menger, Leon Walras, and W. S. Jevons.[5] Similarly, it is difficult to ascertain the relationship between the articulations of the neoclassical perspective in England and Europe in the 1870s and the earlier nineteenth-century contributions of, for example, Cournot and Dupuit in France and Thünen, Mangoldt, and Gossen in Germany. However, while these earlier economists indeed addressed key aspects of the neoclassical emphasis on microeconomic marginal utility, our story begins sometime in the 1870s, the decade in which appeared Carl Menger's *Principles of Economics* (1871), W. S. Jevons' *Theory of Political Economy* (also 1871), and Leon Walras's *Principles of Economics* (1874). Although they were unaware of each other's efforts, these economists were working simultaneously on a number of the same unresolved problems facing the field, and they arrived at a remarkable disciplinary convergence.[6] Between 1871 and the early decades of the twentieth century, the work of these and other neoclassical economists such as Alfred Marshall in England, Vilfredo Pareto in Switzerland, Eugen Böhm-Bawerk in Austria, and John Bates Clark in the United States marked the continued development of this change in mainstream economic analysis.[7]

A number of key points can be made about the direction of their work. First, they tended toward an even more formal and rigorous methodology than did their classical predecessors, which was perhaps not unrelated to the increasing desire to professionalize their discipline (a widespread phenomenon in many academic fields at that time). For example, they came to deploy mathematical models (such as differential calculus) much more ambitiously, and they further attempted to effect the transformation of "political economy" into "economic science" by divorcing (or at least distinguishing) their discipline from political science, history, philosophy, and law. Instead, economists such as Jevons repeatedly invoked physics (or "mechanics") as a disciplinary model for the sort of rigor and "purity" he sought.[8] This change was accompanied by a shift from the classical emphasis on macroeconomic production, distribution, and growth toward microeconomic models of specific market scenarios, the actions of individual economic agents within those markets, and the implications of these microeconomic configurations for the broader social welfare. One difference, then, between classical and neoclassical economics is approximately replicated in the more familiar contemporary distinction between macroeconomics and microeconomics. The individual, as it were, steps more fully into the spotlight on the neoclassical economic stage.

As mentioned above, another key difference involved moving away from a production-cost theory of value. Instead of looking at the costs of production (such as labor) as the source of value of economic goods, neoclassical economists focused on the utility that a good provided an individual consumer. In this move then, two changes can be noted: a shift from production to consumption, and from a broader social framework to a narrower focus on the individual's subjective states, contingent situations, and revealed preferences. Even when neoclassical economists attempted to construct models of either partial or general market equilibria (e.g., Marshall and Walras, respectively), they used this microeconomic analysis as a kind of "ground floor." This model was expressed by means of the techniques of marginal analysis (hence the term "marginalist revolution" that is also widely used to describe this work), which essentially showed how economic behavior could be better grasped in terms of incremental changes in, and relative comparisons of, the choices facing economic agents. Regarding consumption, for example, the utility of a good is determined solely by its position in a system of relative differences (e.g., the relative scarcity of a good and/or its comparison with other goods). The individual consumer makes choices according to these differential comparisons, and these choices in their aggregate make up market demand, which, in turn, plays a role in market price and output.

To take an example: Assume I am trying to decide how much pizza and beer to consume, given my budget and tastes. The utility of pizza and beer are not absolute or fixed quantities. Instead, their utility is determined by my taste for pizza and beer, which is necessarily subjective. Moreover, my taste for pizza and beer is not fixed, as it is linked to objective contingencies as well, such as their relative scarcity and the level of their consumption. The general assumption here is that goods have a greater utility as they are increasingly scarce, just as higher levels of consumption eventually arrive at diminishing marginal returns (and if I really overdo it, diminishing total returns). If the slice of pizza has the same price as a glass of beer, the utility-maximizing consumer choice would be to select a combination of pizza and beer in which the marginal utility (or incremental pleasure) of the *last* slice of pizza equals the marginal utility of the *last* glass of beer. (If the prices are different, then their respective marginal utility/price ratios should be equal.)

Neoclassical economists sought to eliminate what they considered to be the methodological and philosophical morass of classical and Marxist discussions of value by replacing them with this marginal utility analysis, which they argued was more precise as a logical description of economic behavior. They thought, for example, that in the concept of marginal utility they were able to conjoin the dichotomy between use-value and exchange-value that had plagued classical and Marxist theory, since utility signified the usefulness of a good *and* expressed it in a system of exchange with other goods. Similar marginal analysis could be applied to production decisions (involving marginal productivity and costs), and these microeconomic formations, in turn, help build an entire model of economic activity in the marketplace. Marginal analysis, whether looking at consumer utility or production costs, focuses more on relative differences (changes, comparisons, etc.) than on fixed identities. This model, it might be noted, is not unlike that of the linguist Ferdinand de Saussure, the neoclassicals' contemporary whose structuralist model of linguistic meaning also posits identities that are determined by their position in signifying systems of relative differences. Moreover, Saussure noted the similarity between this ahistorical and abstract model of economic value and his own approach to linguistics. (I discuss this formal and historical coincidence in more depth in Chapter 5 on *Sister Carrie*.)

To sum up, several key aspects of the neoclassical approach to keep in mind are its microeconomic focus on the individual economic agent, its formal abstraction of that microeconomic agent as a utility maximizer, and its deployment of marginal analysis to describe economic behavior in many areas of economic activity in order construct a model of market equilibrium. There is of course much more to be said about both classical and neoclassical economics, and in each of the ensuing chapters, these and other aspects are taken up at more length and explained in more detail, since it is assumed that specific economic concepts will be more meaningfully grasped—and their relation to literary study of the novel more fully appreciated—if those concepts are elaborated in close connection with the four novels and their critical reception.

III. CRITICAL COINCIDENCES AND OVERSIGHTS

As noted above, contemporary literary criticism makes use of Marxist concepts more than it draws upon mainstream classical and especially neoclassical analysis, and (Foucault's paddling pool notwithstanding) one would expect that this choice of economic referents would affect critical reading practices. After all, Marxist and neoclassical analysis proceed along significantly different sets of methodological assumptions, formal concepts, and rhetorical purposes.[9] Neoclassical analysis begins with individual endowments and preferences, as opposed to the class struggle between capital and labor. It tends to localize and abstract economic scenarios, as opposed to historicizing them in a broad set of social conditions. It tracks the efficiency and equity of allocative and distributional mechanisms of different market structures (such as perfectly competitive and monopolistic scenarios), as opposed to the exploitation of labor by capital. It does not propose a teleological account of long-term strain and collapse from capital accumulation, but a tendency toward market equilibrium for a given a set of conditions that are themselves subject to constant change and disruption. It does not speak of commodification, reification, or alienation. It does not engage in critique, in the Marxist sense. To a Marxist, neoclassical analysis is, as it were, both all too familiar and completely foreign.

Perhaps the relative scarcity of neoclassical analysis in economic interpretations of literature could be explained as a problem of increasing professionalization and specialization, in which the formal, technical aspects of this economic discourse has kept literary critics at a distance (not that Marx is an easy read). It might also be explained in ideological terms, in which the coincidence between mainstream market discourse and novelistic fiction is taken for granted (e.g., the circulation of bourgeois ideologies of individual agency and subjectivity). For example, as I argue in Chapter 2, Marxist readings of *Robinson Crusoe* tend to note the coincidence between the individualistic tenor of mainstream market economics and Defoe's representation of an island solitary, and then proceed to read that fictional representation as a fib that both expresses one economic formation and represses another. For the novel can be said to tell two stories, one about individualistic economic agency and another in which that individual is located in a historical and economic context of class struggle, international trade, and colonial exchange: Crusoe does commerce, as it were, both within the boundaries and beyond the shores of his solitary economy, in the series of transactions before the shipwreck, on the island, and upon his return. Crusoe both engages in autonomous capital production and realizes capital accumulation by way of a series of economic exchanges, as in his earlier trade adventures, the plundering of the ship's capital (which signifies an earlier economic story), and the ultimate returns of his Brazilian holdings, which have accrued in his absence during his island stay.

Classical and, to a greater extent, neoclassical analysis of capital presents a model of delay, detour, and return that resembles Defoe's depiction of how Crusoe engages in a series of economic strategies of capitalization and material advance that go beyond simplistic claims of capitalist frugality or Marxist exploitation, for this formation of what I refer to as "narrative yield" is intricately scripted into aspects of the novel's economic subject matter, characterological subjectivity and agency, plot structure, and narrative technique. For example, Crusoe's journal is itself a performance of this joint-production between literary and economic production, in which the structures and strategies of narration are tied to both economic production and the production of a textual self in such a way as to point to a coincidence between economic, psychological, and textual delays, detours, and returns. And while this coincidence has been noted in economic readings of the novel, previous interpretations have failed to consider how mainstream economic representations of capital offer a model for this relation between novelistic form and content. For example, Peter Hulme reads psychological and textual formations of delay, detour, and return as fictional productions that repress the economic realities of capitalist and colonialist exploitation, whereas I argue that they express a version of economic production that better reveals the "coincidence of wants" between economic discourse and novelistic fiction. While some readers might wish to return to a critique of this coincidence from a Marxist perspective, they could perhaps more productively do so by way of a neoclassical detour. Even so, this coincidence might produce a different reading of the novel's economic elements—as well as their relation to other non-economic aspects. Perhaps, for example, we need not read Crusoe's formations of detour and delay strictly as psychological and textual fabrications whose relation to the economic "truth" is to be rendered only in terms of a series of somewhat ironically self-fulfilling distinctions between fictional and economic production.

So, while readings that deploy neoclassical concepts can present a number of affinities with Marxist interpretations of exchange between economics and novelistic form and content, these coincidences nevertheless often point to important differences. A second example both underscores this point and introduces my analysis of Mary Shelley's *Frankenstein* in Chapter 3. Marxist interpretations of this novel tend to read the relation between Victor and the monster in terms of the central

Marxist concept of the conflict between capital and labor, in which Victor and the monster are said to occupy either chair in a variety of Marxist seating arrangements (Victor, for example, has been read both as a capitalist who abhors his production of the proletariat monster, and as a laborer who is alienated by the modes of capitalist production). This economic relation, in turn, is said to be both expressed as, and repressed by, a fictional fabrication in which real economic conditions are rendered as a kind of romance of gothic transmogrification.

However, the trajectory of classical and neoclassical analysis not only rejects this dualistic model of the struggle between capital and labor, but increasingly articulates the agency and function of a distinct economic identity that can find no quarter in the Marxist story—the entrepreneur. A distinction is made in mainstream analysis between the capitalist, who merely possesses capital, and the entrepreneur, who creatively recombines the other factors of production (capital, labor, and land) and animates them into innovative and risk-taking configurations. A reading of Victor as an entrepreneur innovatively animates a number of interpretive possibilities. First, it underscores a self-reflexive relation between Shelley's own description of her literary enterprise and Victor's undertaking of "filthy creation." Second, it provides a way of reading the representation of individual creativity and risk in the story in economic terms quite different from the Marxist focus on production and alienation, neither of which adequately describes Victor's own account (or the reader's experience) of his objective predicaments and subjective states. These include the element of uncertainty, the ambivalence about the realization of innovative outcomes, and his rather extreme bipolar emotional swings in which dread and desire are linked to both success and failure. Third, economic representations of the "creative destruction" of the entrepreneur resonate with romantic figurations of the solitary hero who is doomed to a kind of failure or dissolution, in which market forces either reject the entrepreneurial innovation as a kind of monster *or* naturalize it, as secrets are revealed, patents expire, monopolies give way, competition rises, and "supranormal" profits are eliminated. Not only does this entrepreneurial narrative delineate a number of aspects of Victor's predicament, but it also speaks to the ambiguities and ambivalences of Shelley's gothic production of that predicament. For this gothic story is not a determined account of economic production, nor is it just a literal depiction of the entrepreneur, but a fictional performance of the animated disturbances of individual creativity, risk, and innovation as they are represented in economic discourse.

Again, both the similarities and the differences between Marxist readings and mine should be apparent. For while the former have usefully brought to our attention the economic content in the novel (e.g., the role of wealth, the patterns of enterprise, and colonialism), they do not conjoin this content with Shelley's mode of gothic production, except to do so by rather ironically reifying a differentiation between economic and literary production. As with *Robinson Crusoe*, a neoclassical heuristic can serve Marxist critical purposes, insofar as an entrepreneurial reading of *Frankenstein* points to a coincidence between economic discourse and Shelley's fiction that could be put into a framework of Marxist critique (gothic romance as entrepreneurial ideology). Yet this coincidence itself animates a number of disturbances regarding the applications and capacities of the Marxist concepts of capital and labor as reading tropes, as well as the ability of the Marxist approach to put forth a relation between economic and novelistic representation beyond the determined claim about fictional formations as the repression and displacement of an economic content. Previous Marxist readings necessarily overlook precisely those characteristics that constitute the conditions of this gothic production—or banish them as fictional monstrosities capable of being recognized only as naturalized Marxist identities.

It would indeed be an oversimplification to pose these differences and disagreements solely in terms of Marxist vs. non-Marxist economic perspectives. For example, New Historicist critics often give great attention to economics in general, and while many Marxist critics have challenged New Historicist critics as dabblers in both history and economics whose postmodern pastiches undermine the possibilities of oppositional critique, other critics have argued that New Historicists make too much of the economic determinations of literature. Indeed, New Historicism is an interesting site for mapping out the contemporary critical landscape, as it is a hybrid composed of many critical practices and theoretical positions.[10] Similarly, the practitioners and productions of the New Economic criticism (which has links to the New Historicism) are so heterogeneous as to make problematic any neat description, but they reflect the broad interdisciplinary interest in reassessing the relationship between economic and literary discourse.[11]

Five cursory examples by Kurt Heinzelman, David Kaufmann, John Vernon, Walter Benn Michaels, and James Thompson reflect both the range and pattern of recent economic criticism, especially in their introductory remarks and theoretical self-positioning. Moreover, this short survey helps to contextualize my own approach, for while they all deploy a similar poststructuralist model of coincidence and exchange between economic and literary discourse, they make no reference to neoclassical analysis. Since all but Heinzelman discuss either the novels or the particular economic concepts that I examine in the following chapters, the consequences of this neoclassical absence are more readily apparent.

I begin with Heinzelman because *The Economics of the Imagination*, published in 1980, is one of the earliest and most widely cited works in surveys of contemporary economic criticism. Heinzelman begins by suggesting that the Greek *oikonomia* (management of the household) offers a useful trope for exploring the relation between literary and economic representation: "In its largest sense, the word asserts our capacity for creating intellectual structures and for imaginatively regulating them" (ix). Moreover, Heinzelman seeks to resist easy mimetic or causal models of the nature of this exchange between economics and literature, for his approach

> is, rather, an intersystemic analysis of the language and logic which poetic and economic 'systems' share. More specifically, by determining how economic theory imaginatively—fictively—structures economic discourse, we may explore how the art of political economy incorporates these structures; how this art is then expressed, formulated, and reassessed in literature; and how it is also transfigured there. (xi)

Heinzelman later states:

> the economic complicity of literature is integrally connected to the discursive complexity of economics. The literature . . . prompts us to understand economics itself as an imaginative event, forming what could be regarded as a counterpoetics, and supplying our written and oral discourse with a linguistically rich, ethically ambiguous, but mythically resonant system of metaphor. (9)

Much of Heinzelman's book is given over to surveying how this connection between economics and literature is variously reflected in economic discourse, literary texts, psychoanalysis, and linguistics. In addition to its poststructuralist inflections, his approach reflects two common characteristics in much of the contemporary analysis of literature and economics: First, his discussion of non-Marxist mainstream political economy is mostly confined to classical theory. While this is perhaps predictable and appropriate, given the historical and cultural proximities of classical political economy and Romantic poetry (the literature on which he focuses), Heinzelman is also clearly attempting to suggest a much less locally determined and historically bound connection between economic and literary discourse. Yet in doing so he largely ignores the neoclassical elaboration of classical theory. Perhaps this is due, in part, to the second feature of Heinzelman's approach, in which concepts from Marxist and classical economics are variously combined to produce readings of specific literary texts. For example, Heinzelman discusses Wordsworth's poetry and criticism in terms of a series of analogies between reader-response theory and classical and Marxist labor theories of value (reader as laborer). Yet one could make the argument that it is neoclassical analysis, with its shift toward a more subjective and contingent notion of value based on individual utility consumption, that offers a better metaphor for reader-response theory and romantic notions of literary values and individual subjectivity. Conversely, reference to the neoclassical model would tend to highlight the degree to which those perspectives present themselves in earlier classical analysis as well. Heinzelman's critical forking in the road, in which Marxist discourse is conjoined with the classical perspective, while the development of neoclassical analysis is largely ignored, is both fairly common and somewhat problematic, insofar as he argues for going beyond a strictly local and determined account of exchange between literary and economic discourse.

A second example involving romantic literature and classical political economy further underscores this contemporary critical pattern, for David Kaufmann's *The Business of Common Life: Novels and Classical Economics between Revolution and Reform* also reflects a number of these protocols in recent poststructuralist economic interpretation. First, much like Heinzelman, his discussion of mainstream political economy is limited to the classical period and the literature produced in England in the early years of the nineteenth century (Kaufmann discusses fiction by Shelley, Radcliffe, Scott, and Austen). Yet Kaufmann proposes a relation between economic discourse and literary fiction that is more than a strictly local or direct exchange. Describing his book as a "study of liberalism," Kaufmann argues that to "construct a history of liberalism one really should read . . . novels" (vii). Primarily interested in how liberalism negotiates "commutative rights and distributive justice" in the pursuit of "happiness" in a market society, Kaufmann argues that both the novel and classical political economy were two key discourses in the business of "legitimating modernity" (viii-ix). Kaufmann explores a number of connections between classical political economy and novelistic fiction—their rising legitimacy, their similar subject matter, and the parallels between state and home economies respectively associated with the spheres of economic discourse and domestic fiction.

Kaufmann's first chapter ("Dialectics, Systems, and Context") opens with this observation:

> There is an odd convergence in late Georgian culture that has generally escaped notice. In the first three decades of the nineteenth-century, political economics became the center of concerted intellectual activity and debate. In this same period, the novel as a genre achieved newfound critical status. In short, economic theory and narrative fiction in prose both became objects of and media for considerable and respectful discussion. (1)

"This concatenation of details," Kaufmann goes on to suggest, "presents problems, not solutions. . . . We are thus prompted to ask how should the fortunes of these disparate spheres be understood to coincide? In other words, can we find a mediation between the two?" (3). In attempting to ascertain the "parallel contributions to the project of framing, expressing, and suppressing the needs generated by the development of British commercial modernity," Kauffman seeks not only to grapple with the nature of the relationship between classical political economy and the novel within the historical frame of early nineteenth-century Britain, but also to address why the works of certain economists and novelists "remain so compelling, so apparently urgent" and "still command such wide readerships" today (4-5). Like many other contemporary critics interested in capitalism and the novel, Kaufmann is attempting to negotiate a complex series of poststructuralist exchanges involving production and reception, economics and literature, and conditions and discourses. Kauffman himself describes his approach as a dialectical one, done in the Hegelian "spirit of contradiction" that he argues crucially informs the contemporary critical landscape, including Lacanian psychoanalysis, deconstruction, Marxism, and postcolonialism (6).

In his conclusion, Kaufmann writes that in order to save his book from the "abstraction of a history of ideas," his analysis focuses on the "impress of immediate political problems and contemporary social questions" of the first three decades of the nineteenth century in Britain. Yet he notes that "behind the historicism that informs . . . this book, there is also a strain of anti-historicism, of hermeneutic recuperation" (170). In other words, he is interested in how the novels and economic analysis of that period retain their "cultural importance to our own day." This broad "coincidence of wants" argues for a connection beyond the confines of early nineteenth-century economics and novels. Accordingly, the neoclassical elaboration of classical market theory, as well as the ongoing development of the novel, points to the possibilities of another project that is more historically comprehensive, discursively inclusive, and hermeneutically recuperative.

Kaufmann reads *Frankenstein* as an important fictional meditation on several of the key issues addressed by the novelist's classical economic contemporaries, such as the tension between commutative rights and distributive justice, which Kaufmann explores in terms of Shelley's ambivalent and ambiguous depiction of the relationship between Victor and the monster—their individual rights, their obligations to each other, and their positions in society more broadly. Moreover, he argues that Shelley's gothic innovation is itself a formal performance of these tensions in capitalistic modernity, such as in the text's many references to earlier pretexts upon which it draws and from which it turns away. Yet as noted earlier, classical and neoclassical articulations of the entrepreneur as an agent of "creative destruction" render this aspect of modernity as a specifically economic configuration of individualistic creativity, risk, and change. Perhaps the entrepreneur does not emerge in Kaufmann's analysis and in other critical readings of *Frankenstein* because the entrepreneur is but a flickering and uncertain identity in pre-classical and classical analysis, and the lineaments of his visage appear more fully only later in neoclassical analysis. Still, as I argue in Chapter 3, tracing that production in pre-classical, classical, and neoclassical analysis offers a way of articulating more comprehensively the "cultural importance" of Shelley's fiction then and now.

A third example of the recent New Economic criticism can be found in John Vernon's *Money and Fiction: Literary Realism in the Nineteenth and Early Twentieth Centuries*, in which he argues that money is the "most habitual obsession" of realistic fiction—and the novel in particular (9), and that this "obsession" is manifest in novelistic form and content, as well as in its historical development. In other words, literary and economic representation are formally analogous, historically linked, and discursively interactive. Noting that money figures importantly in the social conditions that the realistic novel mimetically represents, Vernon attempts to negotiate historical and formal ties that would move a discussion of money beyond its delineation either as merely literal subject matter or as purely allegorical metaphor: "Money in this book stands for both larger economic forces . . . and 'smaller' psychological ones: desire, need, ambition. Like the novel, it functions metonymically, though like the novel it is also a form of representation" (22). Accordingly, Vernon offers a chiasmatic formulation of New Historicist coincidence and exchange: "I deal not so much with causes or determinations as with reciprocity of effect, a mutual qualification of history and form . . . as both unfold" (22). With his model in place, Vernon proceeds to explore connections between money and realism, such as the nineteenth-century debates about metal vs. paper monetary standards and their resemblance to questions about the mimetic possibilities of fiction. Vernon's argument proposes a sort of quantum of exchange between literary and economic discourse, a transaction that itself does collateral business with the historical conditions in which those texts are produced and consumed. Yet no attention is given to formal mainstream classical and neoclassical economic analysis of money.

Vernon and other readers of nineteenth-century American fiction, like so many other readers of literary paper, have been drawn to these evocative questions about monetary materiality, representation, and value. These critics tend to direct our attention to how some relation between fiction and the world resembles a similar connection between money and the economy, especially in terms of analogous sets of questions involving the material stuff of signification and its relation to the real. They consistently underscore the importance of longstanding debates about metal vs. paper monetary standards, and have seen in this discourse a similar problem involving the representational capacities of literary fiction. Yet we need not focus only on this singular aspect of money in our readings of fiction. For while as committed readers of paper (and perhaps a textualized reality) we might indeed be drawn to such controversies about monetary standards, economists have arguably been even more interested in the relationship between money—whatever the material—and it real economic effects on trade.

In my analysis of Herman Melville's *Moby Dick* in Chapter 4, I make reference to this more crucial set of problems in mainstream monetary theory in order to explore Melville's monetized fictional economy, by which I mean how the relationship between novelistic representation and economic reality is rendered in terms of a variety of monetary tropes. In formal economic analysis, a question that is related to, but distinctly different from, the problem of monetary standards has concerned economists at least as far back at the mercantilists of the seventeenth century and as recently as the contemporary monetarist school of "rational expectations": what effect does money—whatever the material form it might take or the inscriptions written upon it—have on "real" economic conditions, such as employment, output, distribution, and consumption? What real difference, as it were, does money make beyond its own representational function of nominally rendering real economic values? Throughout the history of economic thought, we encounter various formulations and related aspects of this question, in which money is said to have a real effect on those conditions and, conversely, to function as an essentially neutral or merely nominal signifier of real economic outcomes. For example, what is the relationship between the money supply and the facilitation of trade? What is the relationship between money supply and prices? Does a change in the money supply merely change price levels, or does it alter real economic outcomes? What are the mechanisms of that material impact?

Melville's novel presents a similar set of questions, insofar as his romantic representation of whaling is linked to monetary figuration. For example, the gold doubloon that Ahab offers the crew as an incentive for sighting Moby Dick can be read as a monetary figure by which the value of an economic identity is nominally represented or as that which makes a real difference in the realization of those choices and outcomes. Moreover, the doubloon is itself a site of self-reflexive inquiry into this relation between representation and reality, thereby suggesting a link between monetary and romantic representation: the doubloon raises the "price" of the whale in a way that is not entirely set apart from what could be described as the metaphysical inflation that attends to the signification of the doubloon. Similarly, the whale is itself a kind of monetized commodity insofar as, like gold, it is an economic commodity that is also a central signifier of economic and romantic values, and it is thus much like the doubloon Ahab introduces into the Pequod's economy. Here again, the question is whether this monetized representation of the whale reflects a system of romantic nominalization that makes any real difference in economic outcomes. This is evident, for example, in a complex series of connections in which the gold doubloon and the whale are linked to colonial discourse in the novel, which (again, like money) both represents and realizes an international economy that is romantically nominalized as a kind of universal household. The world girdled with guineas that Ahab scorns is not entirely disconnected from the doubloned economy in which he would participate and by which Melville invites us to dip our hands into the "delicious mollifier" of whaling rendered as romance. Money, like Melville's romance, oils the wheels of trade, and in doing so, is something of a wheel in its own right.

The jump from Melville's doublooned romance to the naturalist purchases of *Sister Carrie* is perhaps not so large when one keeps in mind the extent to which these novels both make use of economic subject matter and then integrate and implicate that material with other aspects of fictional form and content. In their readings of Theodore Dreiser's novel, critics have widely addressed Dreiser's pervasive preoccupation with desire, and have variously linked it both to his novelistic technique and to his economic subject matter. Walter Benn Michaels' analysis of *Sister Carrie* in *The Gold Standard and the Logic of Naturalism* serves as a useful example of the recent critical reception of this novel in particular, as well as the more general similarities and differences between previous economic reading practices and my own.

Michaels' analysis of the relationship between capitalism and Dreiser's naturalist fiction is organized around a poststructuralist model of what he calls a "principle of discrepancy" in the novel. In order to formulate this as an economic configuration, Michaels explores both classical and Marxist theories of value, arguing that in Smith's, Ricardo's, and Marx's works, tropes of "identity by difference" similarly organize their respective analyses of monetary, commodity, and labor value. These economic values are identities that, according to Michaels, are never quite at one with themselves, for they have meaning only in systems of difference (e.g., use-value rendered as exchange-value), a formulation that he finds useful in addressing naturalist representation from a poststructuralist perspective. That is, Michaels reads elements of fictional form and content not only as analogous configurations of an economic problematic, but as literary productions that actively participate in the discourses and conditions of capitalism. Michaels sets up a series of analogous formations of identity and difference in economic discourse in order to propose that naturalist fiction, like the capitalist marketplace, has a vested interest in producing human subjects whose identities are formulated in the difference between what one is and is not, or more specifically, between what one has and what one desires to possess.

Michaels' argument is too complicated to describe and assess here, but a number of salient points can be made. Michaels' analysis combines classical and Marxist theories of value, but entirely overlooks neoclassical analysis. Ironically, his discussion of nineteenth-century economic representations of identity, value, and difference makes no reference to the profound shift in the way economists theorized value around the time of the publication of *Sister Carrie*, although the neoclassical version of the individual consumer whose subjective desire is signified in a system of relative differences resonates with Michaels' analysis of desire in Dreiser's novel. However, while a consideration of neoclassical analysis yields a number of important similarities with—and even a certain corroboration of—Michaels' analysis, it also points to some problems in Michaels' and other critics' claims about economic and naturalist representations of desire in *Sister Carrie*.

For example, Michaels and other critics read Carrie's desire as a kind of engine of Dreiser's fictional economy and the force that sustains the capitalist economy represented there, while the absence of desire, as represented by Hurstwood's indifference, signifies either a threat to, or failure of, market capitalism (Michaels goes on to argue that naturalist narrative has a similar stake in desire, in which satisfaction is a kind of entropic death that shuts down both economic and narrative activity). Carrie's desire is structured and sustained by comparisons between what she is and what she is not, between commodities she both possesses and wants to possess, and between a number of people with whom she enters into a series of personal and economic relationships. At the same time, however, Michaels (and other critics) argue that Hurstwood eventually stands outside this naturalist/poststructuralist logic, just as he increasingly finds himself outside the real market economy.

Yet Dreiser's representation of indifference (a word that appears about fifty times in the novel, depending on which version you read) "carries" desire in a way that resists this dualistic formulation. Rather than arguing for an oppositional relation between desire and indifference—and an analogous set of economic and literary distinctions, I examine how Dreiser's naturalistic representation of indifference does not mark the absence of, or resistance to, desire, but instead structures and sustains desire in the fictional economy of the novel. In this neoclassical model, the concept of indifference marks the path along which the desiring consumer proceeds as she makes utility-maximizing choices by comparing differences in utility. Indifference is, as it were, the delineation of desire along lines of difference. And because desire is alive and well in this neoclassical representation of indifference, it therefore usefully helps us to revise our account of their relation in *Sister Carrie*, for indifference is always in some sort of play with desire in Dreiser's fictional economy. Neoclassical utility theory delineates a "principle of discrepancy" somewhat as Michaels argues, yet it allows us to put indifference back into that representational system, rather than seeing it as a world apart from the poststructuralist logic of consumer desire. In other words, neoclassical analysis presents a certain concurrence with Michaels' economic reading of desire, even as it challenges this problematic New Historicist blend of poststructuralist play and Marxist work.

I wish to conclude by referring to a critic whose work is the most recently published of these examples, who articulates quite effectively a rationale for linking political economy and the novel, and whose discussion of Defoe both anticipates where I begin in the next chapter and reflects the pattern of critical oversight regarding neoclassical analysis. James Thompson's *Models of Value: Eighteenth-Century Political Economy and the Novel* offers a number of evocative connections between novelistic and economic discourse. He suggests that in "eighteenth-century England, both political economy and the novel grow out of concerns with value and variables, as they develop the mathematical and narrative technology of 'what if. . . .'" (2). He proposes that "novelistic narrative is a historically specific form of storytelling whose specificity is determined by a stage in the development of capital" (7) and then poses a poststructuralist quantum of coincidence not unlike mine or that of the other critics' cited here:

> the interrelation between the development of the novel and economic change has to be understood not as determinate or reflective or mimetic—not as base and superstructure—but rather as mediated by the concurrent development of political economy as a discourse and the novel as a discourse. (8)

Thompson provides both an evocative theoretical stance and a productive reading of how the novel and political economy reflect and construct models of value that variously inform one another. However, he makes a move not unlike the one noted repeatedly above: the tendency to synthesize classical and Marxist concepts and to ignore neoclassical ones. For example, Thompson discusses capital accumulation in Defoe's fiction largely by conflating the concepts of money and capital in a way that, while deploying a Marxist perspective that generates some compelling insights, presents three related problems: first, he overlooks the key distinction between these terms in the classical literature such as Smith's *Wealth of Nations*; second, he makes no reference to how neoclassical economists elaborated on a number of key aspects of classical analysis of capital; and third, as a result, he overlooks important elements in Defoe's representation of capital accumulation in the fiction.

So, I turn now to *Robinson Crusoe* to explore in more depth both the critical indifference to neoclassical analysis and the difference it can make in our reading of the novel and our understanding of its relation to political economy.

NOTES

[1] Just about any history of the novel will make direct or indirect reference to conditions, attitudes, and practices related to economics. Some examples of this tradition are Nancy Armstrong, *Desire and Domestic Fiction: A Political History of the Novel*; M. M. Bahktin, *The Dialogic Imagination*; Cathy N. Davidson, *Revolution and the Word: The Rise of the Novel in America*; Georg Lukács, *Theory of the Novel*; Michael McKeon, *The Origins of the English Novel 1600-1740*; Edward W. Said, *Beginnings: Intention and Method*; James Thompson, *Models of Value: Eighteenth-Century Political Economy and the Novel*; Ian Watt, *Rise of the Novel: Studies in Defoe, Richardson, and Fielding*.

[2] While this list might feel like a description biased toward the classical British realist novel of the nineteenth century, which is often distinguished from American romance, for example, I believe these characteristics still serve as broad useful references in comparing the genre with other earlier forms of narrative, such as the ancient epics or medieval romances.

[3] See, for example, Maximillian E. Novak, *Economics and the Fiction of Daniel Defoe*, and John J. Richetti, *Daniel Defoe*. This topic is discussed at more length in Chapter 2 on *Robinson Crusoe*.

[4] See Joseph E. Schumpeter, *History of Economic Analysis*, 181-6.

[5] Also, historicist and socialist challenges to classical dogma increased in this period, as did disagreement within the classical ranks, as is evident in Mill's eventual rejection of the wages-fund doctrine.

[6] For a short but useful assessment of the "marginalist revolution," see Mark Blaug, *Economic Theory in Retrospect*, 294-328, although just about every history of economic thought takes this problem up (see also Schumpeter, 825-9, 909-920). See John F. Henry, *The Making of Neoclassical Economics*, for a critical Marxist account of what he calls capitalist and scientific "fraud" in the development of neoclassical theory.

[7] This list is by no means complete. For example, any discussion of neoclassical theory ought to include the names Irving Fisher, Knut Wicksell, and A. C. Pigou, who did important work in monetary theory. Morever, the Austrian school

economists, such as Joseph Schumpeter and F. A. Hayek, have close ties with neoclassicism.

[8] For an analysis of how the neoclassical marginalists were influenced by other disciplines, see Philip Mirowski, *More Heat than Light: Economics as Social Physics: Physics as Nature's Economics*, which is an interesting argument about how neoclassical economists literally "lifted" the methodology of mechanistic physics, his point being that it was both bad physics and bad economics (he argues for an institutionalist approach).

[9] For a good comparative overview, see Richard D. Wolff and Stephen A. Resnick, *Economics: Marxian versus Neoclassical.*

[10] For a survey of the New Historicism, see Aram H. Veeser, ed., *The New Historicism*.

[11] This work involves interdisciplinary exchange among literary critics, rhetoricians, and economists, and has generated a number of conferences, articles, and books. For example, in October 1994 The Society for Critical Exchange sponsored a national conference in Cleveland, Ohio, entitled *The New Economic Criticism*, which brought together academics from each of these disciplines. See, for example, Donald N. McCloskey, *The Rhetoric of Economics* and *If You're So Smart: The Narrative of Economic Expertise* for an economist's perspective on the figurative, narrative and rhetorical aspects of economic discourse (McCloskey has been an important figure in this interdisciplinary exchange). For a collection of essays from several disciplines, see Arlo Klamer, Donald A. McCloskey, and Robert M. Solow, eds., *The Consequences of Economic Rhetoric*.

CHAPTER 2

Bound and Unbound

Capital and Narrative Yield in *Robinson Crusoe*

> *"This, then, was the complete game—disappearance and return."*
>
> —SIGMUND FREUD, *BEYOND THE PLEASURE PRINCIPLE* (9)

> *"a greater result is obtained by producing goods in roundabout ways than by producing them directly."*
>
> —EUGEN V. BÖHM-BAWERK, *THE POSITIVE THEORY OF CAPITAL* (19)

> *"As I imagin'd, so it was."*
>
> —*ROBINSON CRUSOE* (42)

I. A PIECE OF ROPE

When Crusoe initially takes stock of his "dreadful Deliverance" on the island, he believes that he is without the necessary resources for survival for even a night and a day:

> I . . . had no Clothes to shift me, nor any thing either to eat or drink . . . neither did I see any Prospect before me, but that of perishing of Hunger, or being devour'd by Beasts . . . I had no Weapon either to hunt and kill any Creature for my Sustenance, or to defend myself . . . In a Word, I had nothing about me but a Knife, a Tobacco-pipe, and a little Tobacco in a Box, this was all my Provision, and this threw me into terrible Agonies of Mind, that for a while I run about like a Mad-man. (39)

Crusoe's "Remedy" is to climb up into a tree and resolve "to sit all Night and consider the next Day what Death I should dye" (39). But the next day the ape-like "Mad-man" is transformed into *homo economicus*.

This transformation is made possible by something more than the presence of the ship. More precisely, this change is produced by a narrative technique in which the ship is first imagined as an absence and then realized as a presence. In that first day of mad despair, Crusoe casts his eye at the "Breach and Froth of the Sea" that isolates him from the "stranded Vessel," which lies so far off that he can hardly see it (39). The ship, then, is first bound in a configuration of separation and lack, which reinforces Crusoe's sense of trauma. But the next day the storm abates, the weather clears, and "the Sea did not rage and swell as before" (40). Thus occurs the first production on the island of a narrative surprise: "that which surpris'd me most, was, that the Ship was lifted off in the Night from the Sand where she lay, by the Swelling of the Tyde, and was driven up almost as far as the Rock which I first mention'd" (40). The ship is returned to Crusoe after the delay of a day and its short detour bound in the sand. This narrative surprise is also an economic return, for the ship contains the capital that allows Crusoe to come down from the tree and to return to a civilized state of *homo economicus*.

And yet not quite. That is to say, not before more delay, detour, and return, for the delivery of the ship is not a done deal. Crusoe says, "I wish'd my self on board, that, at least, I might save some necessary things for my use" (40), and the realization of the wish is again similarly produced in the narrative economy:

> when I came to the Ship, my Difficulty was still greater to know how to get on board, for as she lay a ground, and high out of the Water, there was nothing within my Reach to lay hold of, I swam round her twice, and the second Time I spy'd a small Piece of Rope, which I wonder'd I did not see at first, hang down by the Fore-Chains so low, as that with great Difficulty I got hold of it, and by the help of that Rope, got up into the Forecastle of the Ship. (40)

The rope is the instrument by which Crusoe grabs hold of the economic return(s) of the ship. Yet why this curious little performance of the twice-absent rope, the double-detour around the ship, and his return to the site of its wondrous production? How does this second narrative surprise, like the reappearance of the ship, suggest a connection between narrative technique and economic subject matter in *Robinson Crusoe*? And how does this pattern of delay, detour, and return provide the clue to that connection?

Like Crusoe, critics have taken their turns around the ship, primarily reading it as either a sign of Providential deliverance or the key to capitalist accumulation—or some combination of both (or repudiation of them, such as by casting it as a fantastic production of psychological wish-fulfillment). For example, critics such as G. A. Starr, J. Paul Hunter, and Michael White have argued that this is a soteriological story best understood in terms of the tradition of spiritual autobiography, in which Crusoe's mishaps and deliverances are the recorded manifestations of Providential design involving one pilgrim's progress. Conversely, critics such as Ian Watt, Stephen Hymer, and Richard Braverman have emphasized the secular story of Crusoe's economic predicament, in which the hand of Providence has been replaced by the material and discursive registrations of capitalism. Other critics such as Maxmillian Novak, John L. Richetti, Michael McKeon, and Peter Hulme have sought to link the spiritual and economic discourses, variously arguing for their joint-production as social, philosophical, and psychological formations. These different interpretive positions reflect some of the many lines by which critics have taken hold of the delivery of the goods in *Robinson Crusoe*, with much of the attention given to the relationship between narrative form and content. For example, spiritual readings typically interpret Crusoe's journal as a textual performance in keeping with the tradition of introspective Puritan diary-keeping, whereas economic readings emphasize its secularity, its empirical and individualistic tenor, and its tallying of material stores and economic progress. Psychoanalytic approaches generally note the formal analogies between textual, material, and psychological formations, in which the journal entails various ruptures, discrepancies, repetitions, and wish-fulfillments that constitute a narrative performance of Crusoe's subjective states.

But before the journal there must be ink, and for the ink we must return to the ship, a site where readers of *Robinson Crusoe* have overlooked one interesting line of coincidence between novelistic form and content: how Crusoe's narration formally produces the ship much as Crusoe makes use of the ship's contents throughout the story. For the ship is realized in a narrative configuration of delay, detour, and return that formally anticipates how Crusoe will himself effect his material progress. This coincidence of what I refer to as narrative and economic yield points to a similar configuration in mainstream economic analyses of capital, in which capital is itself both cause and effect of economic advance produced in a roundabout fashion. Classical and neoclassical economic models of capital therefore offer a useful trope for the formations of delay, detour, and return that constitute the narrative technique and economic subject matter of *Robinson Crusoe*.

Several definitions, distinctions, and disclaimers are helpful as an introduction to this argument. First, in my analysis of capital in mainstream economic analysis in relation to Defoe's novel, I am using the term in a much more specific sense than do those readings that use the term to mean any kind of economic asset. Indeed, a pattern in previous critical discussions of capital in *Robinson Crusoe* specifically or the novel genre more broadly is that they tend either to proceed from a Marxist view of capital or to conflate capital with wealth or money—approaches that overlook attempts in the mainstream market tradition to define capital. To take one recent example, in *Models of Value: Eighteenth-Century Political Economy and the Novel*, John Thompson argues for a connection not unlike my own between political economy and the novel; however, while he also uses capital as a link, he really wants to read capital almost exclusively in monetary terms:

> political economy and the novel [are] historically concurrent kinds of description. . . . novelistic narrative is a historically specific form of storytelling whose specificity is determined by a stage in the development of capital, and I detail that stage by looking closely at the advent of paper money and its consequences for both theories of value and theories of representation. (7)

Thompson goes on to describe "the age of the novel . . . confronting money as capital, no longer as treasure, but as money in motion, where the dynamism of capitalist exchange can be linked to narratives of change, transformation, and development" (9). And although he argues for the importance of accumulation in Defoe's novels, Thompson's stated interest in capital is really vested in an analysis of monetary value, which is a related but quite distinct set of economic and literary analogues (I discuss money and value in Chapters 4 and 5 respectively).

Capital is generally defined by mainstream economists as a type of good that is produced to produce more goods. Capital is therefore sometimes referred to as an "intermediate good" because it is a produced good that is itself not a "final" consumable, but is instead employed as a means of further production. It represents a choice whereby instead of expending economic resources for nonproductive consumption now, those resources are directed into the production of productive capacities that generate returns in the future that would otherwise be unrealized. In a sense, capital is a form of waiting that does work. This realization of a supplementary difference can be arrived at only by a "roundabout" route whereby economic resources are not simply saved or hoarded, but actively invested into the production of a return. Capital is a representation of how an economy goes forward by delay and detour. It is a structure of suspense. In this sense, to capitalize is to narrate. Capital tells us how we tell ourselves how we make an economic story.

Another distinction underscored by reference to mainstream analysis of capital is that Crusoe is not just a saver (or a spender). If he were, there would be a different story to tell—if one at all—for it could be argued that either spending or saving alone would result in his death. That is to say, he both saves and spends by way of a capitalizing strategy of investment and return, and his economic progress therefore involves both holding on and letting go in order to produce a material advance realized in a temporal sequence, an economic progress that resembles the way we often describe the activity of narration itself. Crusoe's widely noted propensity for accumulation tends to overlook how capital formation and growth entails this combination of saving and spending that yields a differential return that would otherwise be unrealized. While Crusoe's bookkeeping, his propensity for building enclosures, and his various island stashes might be cited as indications of a retentive psychological formation that resembles economic hoarding, Crusoe's savings are directed into investments that produce the temporal sequentiation of material advance, as is evident in the narration of his series of trade ventures before the shipwreck, the development of his island economy, and the realization of his off-island Brazilian holdings upon his return. The contents of the ship would not have been enough to sustain him for almost thirty years without some strategies of capitalization—and even if they were, *Robinson Crusoe* would have been a much different story.[1]

A third distinction, to which I give more attention later, is between capital and labor—or more precisely, the tendency in other readings to efface that difference by describing capital as merely labor contained, stored, embodied, or congealed. The Marxist sensibility is apparent here, whereas the mainstream classical and neoclassical tendency to articulate what is different between capital and labor—and what difference this difference makes—underwrites my own interpretation.

A fourth distinction to note here is the one between the capitalist and the entrepreneur in mainstream economic analysis from the eighteenth- to the twentieth-century. As I discuss in the next chapter on *Frankenstein*, in addition to the other factors of production (land, labor, and capital), the entrepreneur is a fourth factor of production who is only partly identified and recognized as a distinct agent or function of production, but he steps forth more fully in neoclassical discourse. Essentially, the capitalist is the owner of the economic resources that the entrepreneur "combines" in creative and risk-taking configurations. Although the identity of both factors may reside in the same person, the functions are nevertheless argued to be different. Yet while previous economic readings of Crusoe variously describe and interpret him as a capitalist and an entrepreneur, they tend to conflate these functions and use the terms interchangeably. The focus of my argument, however, is not to read Crusoe mimetically as an economic agent of either stripe, so much as how the concept of capital and its relation to narrative delay, detour, and return points to connections between novelistic form and economic content. Put differently, I want not so much to argue for character as capitalist as to propose that capital is invested in a broader array of novelistic characteristics.

Nevertheless, a look at the literal depiction of capital formation in Crusoe's initial plundering of the ship's contents should help clarify this model of economic delay, detour, and returns. When he realizes he can reach the ship, Crusoe swims out to it in order to meet his need for "present Subsistence," that is, those items he will need for immediate consumption and survival. But after finding bread and rum, he immediately redirects his focus to the future: "I had indeed enough . . . to spirit me for what was before me: Now I wanted nothing but a Boat to furnish my self with many things which I foresaw would be very necessary to me" (41). Crusoe sets aside his concern for "present Subsistence" to make a raft out of some of the ship's materials. He does so, he says, "with a great deal of Labour and Pains, but hope of furnishing my self with Necessaries, encourag'd me to go beyond what I should have been able to have done upon another Occasion" (41). The production of the raft, then, points to a difference between productive and nonproductive goods, whereby Crusoe increases his productive capacity by delaying the gathering of the present consumables in order to direct his efforts into the realization of capital, which allows him to "store" his labor and increase his ability to "furnish [him]self with Necessaries." In other words, Crusoe not only expends his "Labour and Pains," but specifically routes them into the production of capital, a strategy that, in turn, produces the returns at which he would otherwise be unable to arrive, for he can now load up the raft with food, liquor, and clothes. Crusoe again presents himself with a trade-off between consumer and capital outlay, for he shifts his attentions once more: "I . . . took no more than I wanted for present use, for I had other things which my Eye was more upon," and after a long search he finds the "Carpenter's Chest, which was indeed a very useful Prize . . . and much more valuable than a Ship Loading of Gold would have been at that time" (42). Just as Crusoe's narrative begins with capital, capital begins to narrate the story of his economic advance.

As a novelistic representation of capital, this is apparently a straightforward literal depiction. Yet it presents us with a number of economic and narrative complexities. Since capital is itself a produced good, and Crusoe's chest of tools is clearly such a store of capital, it therefore tells of a previous combination of the factors of production, just as Crusoe's production of the raft is itself narrated as an island reenactment of this earlier economic process. Does Crusoe's island economy, then, begin at the beginning, or does the presence of capital complicate this would-be economic starting point? If we were to sail the ship homeward, as it were, to an earlier story, would it tell of a different tale? If capital always represents the realization of an earlier production, can this story of economic advance ever begin in the absence of capital, or is capital itself somehow the very stuff of this storytelling?

These complexities involving the representation of capital in Defoe's novel in general and in the presence of the ship in particular remind us that simply to equate capital with a store of economic wealth (typically money) or other factors of production (such as labor) or to conflate accumulation with investment is to overlook a number of crucial economic concepts involving the production of Crusoe's economic story—past, present, and future. Accordingly, neither the absence nor the presence of the ship itself adequately articulates the representation of capital in the novel. Economic interpretations of capital in *Robinson Crusoe* have nevertheless tended to fall into one of two categories—those that argue that Crusoe begins at zero and proceeds as one, and those that do not.

In the first view, Crusoe's island beginning is depicted as he originally imagines it himself—on his own, provisioned with nothing, and returned to a primitive economic state. In critical readings of Defoe's novel, fictional revisions of the story, and economic theory, Crusoe has been described as the solitary individual who begins on the island *ex nihilo* and moves forward to a more advanced state of economic well-being. These depictions have often overlooked the presence of the ship. An early instance of this tendency can be found in Jean Jacques

Rousseau's *Emile*, in which it is claimed that Crusoe is "cast ashore on a desolate island, destitute of human assistance, and of mechanical implements."[2] Similarly, Edgar Allan Poe announced that "the idea of man in a state of perfect isolation, although often entertained, was never before so comprehensively carried out."[3] Fictional appropriations, such as J. H. Campe's widely read German version, *Robinson der Jungere* (1779), have also imagined a more pure "zero state" from which Crusoe can begin, for Campe eliminates the plundering of the ship's capital altogether. And finally, economists have often referred to Crusoe, as did the neoclassical economist Eugen V. Böhm-Bawerk in 1888, as "a recluse working absolutely without capital . . . thrown on a lonely shore without either tools or weapons . . . . [who being] without capital . . . must at first support life in the most primitive fashion (101).[4] This view is not limited to neoclassical economists, for as discussed below, Marx also underplays the role of the accumulated capital of the ship in order to read Crusoe as an economic laborer who is not alienated from the modes of production, as are his counterparts in a capitalist economy.

Of course, the forgetting of the ship is often cited in interpretations that oppose this version of a solitary and productive *homo economicus.* In this second view, the initial capital outlay plundered from the ship undermines claims for Crusoe's zero-state autonomy, just as his relations with Friday point to the role of broader colonial configurations in this economic story. Similarly, both the social relations and economic conditions off the island, such as Crusoe's earlier ventures and the realization of his Brazilian investments afterward, are said to undermine any version of an entirely self-contained island-economy narrative. For example, Ian Watt argues for the importance of both the ship and Friday as clues to Crusoe's advance. Other Marxist critics such as Stephen Hymer argue that the "contrast between the economist's Robinson Crusoe and the genuine one mirrors the contrast between the mythical description of international trade in economic textbooks and the actual facts of what happens in the international economy" (13). Similarly, Peter Hulme has stressed the importance of Crusoe's colonial relations both on and off the island, arguing that their textual, psychological, and economic productions contain the "secret of capital" in *Robinson Crusoe*, of which the ship but a kind of mimetic allegory.

We return, then, to the gap between the absence and the presence of the ship—a difference replicated not only in the critical reception of *Robinson Crusoe* but also in the economic analysis of capital as well. Marxist and non-Marxist economists share the view that capital is a crucial component in the economic story of capitalism. Capital delineates the route of economic advance, just as it signifies the differences among those economic histories in which advance is variously realized. Indeed, capital not only informs particular sets of historical conditions but is itself a kind of historiography—or a signifier of the entry into history—that distinguishes "civilized" and "primitive" cultures. I refer here to the capitalist ability to narrate a material advance as a temporal progress, as opposed to some relatively "primitive" state bound to the present. (I address this point later in relation to economic analyses of capital as a distinguishing feature between different societies, as well as how it bears on Crusoe's difference from both his European counterparts and the primitive others.) Yet precisely because capital is an instrument for the realization *and* representation of economic production, Marxist and non-Marxist theories also present some fundamental disagreements about capital.

In terms of Crusoe's ship, for example, all readers would probably agree that it presents Crusoe with a certain productive capacity that would otherwise be unavailable to him, and that it therefore determines the direction of his story to some extent. Yet Marxists would argue that the ship and its contents are the result of an earlier set of economic relations and expropriations, and that as capital the ship represents a structural and temporal embodiment (or "congealment") of labor whose exploitation (the difference between labor's contribution and reward) produces a surplus that makes further capitalist accumulation possible. Capital is, in this view, an economic identity that both expresses and represses labor's essential and fundamental status as the source of production. As noted earlier, however, mainstream classical and neoclassical economists tend to resist reducing capital to labor in quite this way, for they argue that it is precisely the unique temporal and structural capacities of capital that define its economic identity and function as a distinct factor of production. Capital signifies, as it were, the production of an economic story that labor alone cannot produce. Put differently, non-Marxists stress capital's unique instrumental capacities as an economic factor of production, whereas Marxists critique both the economic and the ideological consequences of this relation between capital and labor. And it is here that the rub of ideology leaves its mark on how we read the production of the fictional economy of *Robinson Crusoe*. Does capital accumulate in the difference between an originary gap between labor and its reward, or does it instead involve a number of other differences and exchanges involving the present and the future, production and consumption, and desire and satisfaction? If it somehow does both, can we find this production of capital on Crusoe's island, or must we look beyond these fictional shores? And finally, how do we conceive of this production in relation to both narrative technique and economic subject matter?

In the Marxist view, the tendency of readers to forget the ship would perhaps be a symptom of the non-Marxist failure to explain how capital accumulates in the first place by way of social exchange and exploitation. Accordingly, by insisting on the importance of the ship in Crusoe's story, critics have attempted to show how the fiction of Crusoe's island autonomy both suppresses and expresses the historical reality of capitalism. Yet as already suggested, it is not so clear what the presence of the ship expresses. In terms of both economic and narrative production, the patterns of delay, detour, and return that produce the ship and by which the ship effects a material change on the island might be either the formation of a fib that covers up an economic reality or a narrative performance that reveals one. If we wish to avoid reading *Robinson Crusoe* as so much novelistic paydirt that serves as an all-too-easy fund of mimetic allegory for our claims about capital, we need to improve our understanding of how the economic subject matter and narrative technique yield one another. In other words, we ought not let go of the narrative rope in order to grab hold of the economic stash in a reading of the fictional economy of *Robinson Crusoe*, wherever it is that we might wish to go from there. "As I imagin'd, so it was," Crusoe tells us, and so can we ask how it is imagined and how it therefore comes to be. We can do so by further exploring a story that both Marxist and non-Marxist readings have missed—the formal and thematic coincidences between *Robinson Crusoe* and the non-Marxist mainstream tradition of classical and neoclassical representations of capital.

II. CAPITAL AND NARRATIVE PRODUCTION

As described in Chapter 1, the beginning of the classical period of modern political economy is conventionally linked to the publication of Adam Smith's *Wealth of Nations* in 1776, which inaugurated a tradition of inquiry that continued in the works of such economists as David Ricardo, Thomas Malthus, and John Stuart Mill for almost a century, until economists around the 1870s began to propose some important new approaches to classical market analysis. While this neoclassical approach, in turn, has been variously challenged and revised both within and beyond the mainstream tradition, classical and neoclassical analysis together continue to be of profound influence in the way economics is formally taught and popularly conceived. Literary critics' indifference to this economic tradition and its analysis of capital is especially interesting because of the similarities between mainstream economic models of capital and other non-economic (especially psychoanalytic and linguistic) approaches to narrative delay, detour, and return in novelistic fiction. A short review of this classical and neoclassical tradition generally and its analysis of capital in particular will both clarify the role of capital in Defoe's novel and point the way to a number of coincidences with other narratological models.

Classical economists sought to explain such problems as the source and signification of economic value, the way in which a nation realized economic growth, and the mechanisms for the social distribution of wealth. Generally, they proposed a model of a self-regulating market whose outcomes are determined by the self-interested pursuits of its individual members. The tenor of the classical approach is reflected in Adam Smith's Introduction to *The Wealth of Nations*, in which he outlines his main topics: the difference between nations that arises from the productivity of their labor; the "causes of this improvement . . . and the order, according to which its produce is naturally distributed among the different ranks and conditions of men in the society"; the connection between the "private interests and prejudices of particular orders of men" and "the general welfare of the society"; and the role of "the sovereign, or commonwealth" (10-2). As is evident in his title, Smith's analysis is cast largely in terms of the economy of the nation—a description of its history, an analysis of the formal relations of its parts, and a prescription for the realization of wealth in the future.

While they fundamentally agreed with the classical model of a self-adjusting market, neoclassical economists such as W. S. Jevons, Carl Menger, and Leon Walras went about telling this economic story somewhat differently. For example, the broad historical and social sensibility reflected in Smith's classical analysis of aggregate market structures and processes becomes more formally abstract and oriented toward theorizing the behavior of the individual in relation to more local economic scenarios. This difference loosely approximates the familiar distinction in contemporary parlance between macroeconomics and microeconomics, in which the former involves the study of the economic whole, whereas the latter focuses on specific economic parts—the individual consumer, the single producer, and price and output in particular market configurations, such as perfectly competitive and monopolistic conditions.

This shift presents an interesting relation to the economic interpretation of *Robinson Crusoe*—does he represent a macroeconomic metonym or a microeconomic metaphor? Is he a depiction of an entire market economy or a solitary economic agent? Is he both? While the neoclassical model might be seen as most at home on Crusoe's island, Marxist, classical, and neoclassical economists—and the literary critics who make reference to their concepts—have all read the novel along both lines, in which Crusoe variously represents individual economic agents (e.g., capitalist, entrepreneur, laborer) and the broader historical, social, and economic conditions of capitalism (e.g., class relations, national growth, international colonialism). Crusoe's story does its economic signifying, so to speak, as and for one and all.

A second distinction between classical and neoclassical analysis involves the theory of value. Classical economists generally located economic value in production costs—primarily (albeit problematically) in labor. Yet from Smith to Mill one encounters some attempt to conceive of value in terms of both supply and demand, and thereby to reconcile the discrepancy between the notion of a commodity's "natural" price (reflected in the cost of production) and its market price (reflected in the interaction of supply and demand). While Marxist economists more fully pursued the labor theory of value, neoclassical economists took the other fork and directed their attention to consumption. They sought to understand economic value (hence market price) in terms of the utility a commodity provides to the individual consumer. The analysis of value in terms of objective social costs is revised into a configuration of subjective individual desire, in which the utility of a good as perceived by the individual is determined by both its relative scarcity and its usefulness. Utility, in turn, drives individual choice, consumer demand, and market price and output. In the neoclassical view, for example, the value of Crusoe's supply of ink would be said to arise not from the costs of its production (such as the labor "embodied" in it) but from the utility it signifies for Crusoe, which, as Crusoe himself puts it, is a function of both the ink's scarcity and its usefulness:

> The Nature and Experience of Things dictated to me upon just Reflection, That all the good Things of this World, are no farther good to us, than they are for our Use . . . . I had no room for Desire, except it was of Things which I had not, and they were but Trifles, though indeed of

> great Use to me. . . . I would have given a Handful of [the money] for a Gross of Tobacco-Pipes, or for a Handmill to grind my Corn; nay, I would have given it all for . . . a handful of *Pease* and *Beans*, and a Bottle of Ink . . . . (102)

Here Crusoe anticipates another aspect of the neoclassical approach, in which the utility of a good is determined not as some essential or constant identity, but by its position in a system of relative differences.[5] While Crusoe begins by insisting that the value of a good is tied only to its use-value, he goes on to locate that use-value in a configuration of relative scarcities and trade-offs involving other goods. Accordingly, Crusoe ultimately conceives of value in a system of preferences and choices, in which the utility of a good is determined by its relation to other goods, just as that differential relation is determined by varying subjective states and objective contingencies: "Thus we never see the true State of our Condition, till it is illustrated to us by its Contraries; nor know how to value what we enjoy, but by the want of it" (110). Similarly, he later exclaims, "by what secret differing Springs are the Affections hurry'd about as differing Circumstances present! To Day we love what to Morrow we hate; to Day we seek what to Morrow we shun" (123).

Marxist criticism can also find evidence of its concepts of value in *Robinson Crusoe*. For example, in *Capital* Marx pointed to Crusoe as a novelistic realization of the labor theory of value:

> he [Crusoe] knows that his labour, whatever its form . . . consists of nothing but different modes of human labour. . . . His stock-book contains a list of the objects of utility that belong to him, of the operations necessary for their production; and lastly, of the labour time that definite quantities of those objects have, on an average, cost him. All the relations between Robinson and the objects that form this wealth of his own creation, are here so simple and clear as to be intelligible without exertion . . . . those relations contain all that is essential to the determination of value.[6]

Yet Marxist literary critics have indeed exerted themselves in a number of directions in order to make what they would describe as an opaque fictional economy more intelligible, revising, for example, Marx's distinction between Crusoe's simple economy and the complexities brought about by capitalist modes of production. That is, while Marx argued that "[e]verything produced by [Crusoe] was exclusively the result of his own personal labor, and therefore simply an object of use for himself," Marxist critics have since read the novel in terms of the division of labor, commodity exchange, class exploitation, and capital accumulation (evident in the presence of the ship, Crusoe's relations with Friday, and his off-island ventures). These Marxist critics would therefore suggest that the economic story on the island is not to be realized only as an obvious mimetic depiction of labor's production of use-value (as Marx insisted), but also as a mix of fact and fancy circulating in the fiction in such a way as to require further interpretation and critique. Similarly, Marxist readings might very well affirm the coincidence between Crusoe's discussion of value in *Robinson Crusoe* and mainstream utility theories of value, but it is a nod of a different shake, for they would then proceed to critique those affinities and affiliations as the production of capitalist ideology. This impasse is partly the result of the differences among economic models, but not entirely, as is reflected in the complexities that arise when any economic theory is brought to bear on the interpretation of a novel *and* its relation to some economic reality.

The subject of capital is itself a critical instance of these economic and literary complexities. Although published almost sixty years after *Robinson Crusoe,* Adam Smith's *Wealth of Nations* is a useful starting point for surveying the mainstream tradition of classical and neoclassical analysis of capital in relation to the novel.[7] In Book II of *Wealth of Nations*, Smith addresses the "Nature, Accumulation, and Employment of Stock." He begins with this claim: "In that rude state of society in which there is no division of labor . . . it is not necessary that any stock should be accumulated or stored up beforehand," since "[e]very man endeavors to supply by his own industry his own occasional wants as they occur" (276). This absence of the division of labor, then, is the beginning point from which the story of economic development proceeds. Smith launches his entire analysis of *Wealth of Nations* with the observation that the "effects of the division of labor" result in a benefit to all the members of "a civilized and thriving country" (22), thus his claim "that the accommodation of a European prince does not always so much exceed that of an industrious and frugal peasant, as the accommodation of the latter exceeds that of many an African king, the absolute master of the lives and liberties of ten thousand naked savages" (24).

Crusoe describes himself in relation to each of these positions: he is variously European prince, industrious and frugal peasant, primitive king, and naked savage, depending on his objective conditions, subjective states, and social relations. And just as these different positions are, according to Smith, determined by the absence or presence of the division of labor, so too does this division delineate Crusoe's progress. While Crusoe's solitary state would apparently make the division of labor impossible, this division is realized by Crusoe in at least one sense: he divides a variety of laboring tasks within the economy of himself insofar as his many tasks do not simply involve looking to "his occasional wants as they occur"—however varied they may be—for he also attempts to create stores of capital that go beyond "present subsistence." Crusoe effects a division of labor in order to bring himself into a different kind of relation with time and his material conditions. In other words, the division of labor and capital accumulation as represented in *Robinson Crusoe* do not require social exchange, so much as the ability to step out of a condition of primitive presence, as it were, and enter into a temporal and structural configuration by which he can produce this story of economic advance.

The division of labor and the accumulation of capital are cause and effect of each other. As Smith puts it, "As the accumulation of stock must, in the nature of things, be previous to the division of labour, so labour can be more and more subdivided in proportion only as stock is previously more and more accumulated" (277). Crusoe desires to create a store of capital and so he divides his labor, just as that division makes possible the realization of a store of capital that will remove him from his "rude state" and allow him to realize a "civilized and thriving" advance. Again, Marxists argue that this contradictory beginning can only be explained by a hidden story of social exchange and exploitation, hence their emphasis on the presence of the ship, Crusoe's relations with Friday, and Crusoe's off-island ventures. In this view, the division of labor necessitates social exchange, which generates the exploitation of labor whose expropriated surplus value makes the accumulation of capital possible. But mainstream market theory suggests that the formation of capital entails something other than—or supplemental to—social exchange: a strategy for going forward by producing more than one consumes in the present, and directing that difference into the production of productive goods in order to arrive at a differential return in the future.

For example, Crusoe's task is not just to gather more fruit than he can eat in the present, which would only be useful if he could exchange his surplus fruit for another laborer's surplus production of a different good—or if he could find some way of storing that fruit in time. He indeed does the latter (e.g., drying techniques), and that strategy itself marks the production of a crucial difference, since the fruit is thereby transformed into something more like capital, at least in terms of its increased durability. This transformation, in turn, is both cause and effect of his increased productivity. For Crusoe does enter into a kind of exchange with himself, in which he gathers enough fruit to forego fruit-gathering long enough to switch jobs and create other goods (such as baskets) that will make his future fruit-gathering efforts more efficient, thereby freeing up resources for other productive pursuits and the formation of yet more capital.

Crusoe pursues this strategy repeatedly, in which the factors of production are deployed to go beyond "present subsistence" and "occasional wants." He builds a raft for more efficient commodity transport; constructs an elaborate shelter to keep himself secure from present and future danger; parcels his gunpowder to better insure its long-term viability; constructs a "Magazine" of shelves in the cave to transform his "heap of goods" into a systematic outlay for more efficient organization and access; plunders the ship exhaustively to increase his store of productive timber, iron, sail, and rope; devises drying techniques to better preserve and store the fruit he finds on the other side of the island; makes baskets and pots for improved transport and storage; builds tools for the planting, harvesting, and processing of his barley and rice; and builds a pen to increase his stock of goats. Throughout his stay Crusoe produces a story of economic advance by dividing his labor *and* increasing his store of capital.

That the division of labor and the accumulation of capital are cause and effect of each other is a contradiction that is not so much resolved as narrated in the exchanges into which he enters with himself, in those bargains made between desire and satisfaction, the present and the future, and production and consumption. Moreover, as will be discussed later in regard to the "intermediate" production of the journal and its relation to the "final" version of *Robinson Crusoe*, the narrative is itself shaped by these capitalizing structures and strategies. That is, while the narrative is largely organized as an account of a series of productive efforts, those labors are often directed into investments and returns whose temporal and structural features make it impossible for Crusoe to narrate his story as a linear sequence of presently realized economic activities. Crusoe's capital keeps appearing and disappearing and reappearing in the narrative in a way that resembles the logic of capital itself, in which advance is realized in a formation of delay, detour, and return.

Just as Crusoe's expenditures are not directed solely toward present conditions, Crusoe's propensity for saving and postponement cannot be said to be so static or retentive as to preclude any real interest in production toward the realization of change. As noted earlier, Crusoe is not just a saver but an investor in the production of a differential return. Even if we were to argue that these returns are repeatedly reinvested as to postpone consumption indefinitely, we still encounter something quite different from the bound inertness of saving. There is very little on Crusoe's island that resembles the stash of money he hoards throughout his island stay, and even this "returns" with something like a difference at the end—a store and measure of value that "goes away" and then "comes back" as a valuable return once he himself can return home.

Like *Robinson Crusoe*, Smith's analysis emphasizes "parsimony" as the key to the narrative of capital:

> Capitals are increased by parsimony, and diminished by prodigality and misconduct. . . . Parsimony, and not industry, is the immediate cause of the increase of capital. Industry, indeed, provides the subject which parsimony accumulates. But whatever industry might acquire, if parsimony did not save and store up, the capital would not be greater. (337)

Yet Smith's "parsimony" similarly signifies more than saving, for these savings are necessarily directed into productive investment by someone somewhere. That is, Smith assumes that the stock saved by one individual is the "immediate cause of the increase of capital," for implicit in this claim is that the stock will be presently invested by another for productive purposes: "That portion which he annually saves, as for the sake of the profit it is immediately employed as capital, is consumed in the same manner, and nearly in the same time too . . . . the consumption is the same, but the consumers are different" (338). Smith sees the relation between saving and investment as an identity (savings = investment) that produces a transformational difference, a form of holding on *and* letting go that arrives at a supplemental return.

Many of these aspects of delay, detour, and return are further elaborated in neoclassical theory, which brings us ever closer to Crusoe's island. For example, Eugen V. Böhm-Bawerk's *The Positive Theory of Capital* (1888) presents a similar picture of capital, in which production is a combination of the natural world and human labor toward a desired economic result. However, the most productive route is not the most direct one, for "a greater result is obtained by producing goods in roundabout ways than by producing them directly" (19); that is, production is enhanced by the presence of capital, which he defines as "nothing but a complex of intermediate products which appear on the several stages of the roundabout journey" (22) and which "serve as means to the Acquisition of Goods" (38). Capitalist production can therefore be reduced to neither nature nor labor: "Capital . . . is 'stored-up labor,' but it is something more; it is also stored-up valuable natural power. It is the medium through which the *two* original productive powers exert their instrumentality" (99). Böhm-Bawerk takes Crusoe as his example:

> To put the matter, first of all, in its simplest conceivable terms. Suppose a recluse working absolutely without capital—say some Robinson Crusoe thrown on a lonely shore without either tools or weapons. Being without capital he must at first support life in the most primitive fashion . . . . Now what must happen before he can get possession of his first capital? (101)

Again, economic growth involves more than just saving, for it also requires a re-routing of that difference between production and consumption into productive goods: "To put it generally, he must curtail the immediate consumption of the current period to such a point, that it uses up the produce of fewer (past and present) productive powers than come into existence anew in the same period; he must, in a word, save productive powers" (104).

Similarly, in *The Theory of Political Economy* (1871) the English neoclassical economist W. S. Jevons begins his analysis of capital this way:

> In considering the nature and principles of Capital, we enter a distinct branch of our subject. There is no close or necessary connection between the employment of capital and the processes of exchange. . . . An isolated man like Alexander Selkirk might feel the benefit of a stock of provisions, tools, and other means of facilitating industry, although cut off from traffic with other men. Economics, then, is not solely the science of Exchange or Value: it is also the science of Capitalisation. (222)

Later, he provides this description of capital:

> *whatever improvements in the supply of commodities lengthen the average interval between the moment when labour is exerted and its ultimate result or purpose accomplished, such improvements depend upon*

> *the use of capital*. . . . all employments of capital resolve themselves into the fact of time elapsing between the beginning and end of industry. (228-9)

Yet another example of this neoclassical depiction of the relationship between desire and satisfaction, production and consumption, and the role of time can be found in Alfred Marshall's *Economics* (1890):

> human nature being what it is, we are justified in speaking of the interest on capital as the reward . . . in the waiting for the enjoyment . . . . The sacrifice of present pleasure for the sake of future, has been called *abstinence* by economists. But this term has been misunderstood . . . . the accumulation of wealth has generally been the result of a postponement of enjoyment, or of a *waiting* for it. (232-3)

Note that in these neoclassical descriptions of capital we encounter an emphasis on the predicament of one economic agent (whether an individual or a nation), as opposed to the relation between two or more; a tendency to render capital in terms of a kind of psychological amortization of desire and satisfaction; a formal relation between these subjective states and the objective conditions of capital; and a formulation of this relation as a configuration of delay, detour, and returns.

III. CRITICAL COINCIDENCES OF NARRATIVE YIELD

This economic analysis of capital calls to mind narratological studies of similar formal and thematic configurations in novelistic fiction. Two critics whose works reflect this similarity are Peter Brooks (in *Reading for the Plot: Design and Intention in Narrative*) and Edward W. Said (in *Beginnings: Intention and Method* and *Cultural and Imperialism*). Both critics deploy a mix of psychoanalytic, linguistic, and economic models to explore narrative production in terms that approximate my own description of narrative yield, yet while they point to a connection between narrative form and economic subject matter, they make no reference to mainstream economic analysis as a way of comprehending that relation.

Peter Brooks makes use of what he calls Freud's "masterplot" in *Beyond the Pleasure Principle*. Brooks calls for a "textual energetics" (38) in order improve on structuralist models of narrative that cannot come to terms with the observation that plots "are not simply organizing structures, they are also intentional structures, goal-oriented and forward moving" (12). In *Beyond the Pleasure Principle*, Freud speaks of the attempt to gain mastery over some sense of lack (a psychic wound, a feared absence, etc.) by a return to and repetition of the traumatic scene or event, arguing that the repetitive component of the therapeutic narrative allows the energy to be "bound" into a manageable configuration. Similarly, Brooks addresses the relation between narrative beginnings and endings, as well as the middle spaces between them, that "'dilatory space' of postponement and error—and the kinds of vacillation between illumination and blindness that we find there" (96). For Brooks, the Freudian economy of "disappearance and return" is analogous to those

> perceptible form[s] . . . repetition, repeat, recall, symmetry, all these journeys back in the text, return to and returns of, that allow us to bind one textual moment to another . . . . Textual energy, all that is aroused into expectancy and possibility in a text, can become usable by plot only when it has been bound or formalized. . . . To speak of 'binding' in a literary text is thus to speak of any of the formalizations, blatant or subtle, that force us to recognize sameness within difference . . . . they create a delay, a postponement in the discharge of energy, a turning back from immediate pleasure, to ensure that the ultimate pleasurable discharge will be more complete. (101-2)

Freud's psychoanalytic model is quite similar to his contemporaries' neoclassical economic analyses of capital, whereby a kind of economic mastery is realized in terms of a system of delays, detours, and returns in which productive capacities are bound in temporal and structural configurations of lack or absence so that they can return as a supplementary difference. This is something like an economic version of the *fort* and *da* of the child with his string that Freud observes and takes as his model. Indeed, Freud describes his entire approach in *Beyond the Pleasure Principle* as an "economic" one (1).

Similarly, Brooks' formal description of fictional narrative, as well as his attempt to place the novel in an historical context, points to a suggestive coincidence involving literary, economic, and psychoanalytic formations of deferral and advance. Throughout his analysis, Brooks offers indirect connections between fictional narrative and political economy: he points to the parallel between the rise of the novel and the desire for cohesive systems of narrative in the social sciences since the mid-eighteenth century (5); he speaks of the "ambitious heroes of the nineteenth-century novel . . . [who] may be regularly conceived as 'desiring machines' whose presence in the text creates and sustains narrative movement through the forward march of desire" (39); and he points to the correspondence between Freudian discourse and turn-of-the-century physics (42), both of which have suggestive links with subjective and mechanistic aspects of neoclassical theory.[8]

Although Brooks does not discuss *Robinson Crusoe*, his model can be easily put to work there. Crusoe's series of trade ventures before the shipwreck, for example, not only corroborate Brooks' analysis, but also underscore how these narrative formations are tied to economic subject matter. On Crusoe's first trip at sea the ship almost founders in a storm, but the foul weather clears, the sailors celebrate by getting drunk, and in those spirits Crusoe's vows of repentance and resolution are "drowned" away (10). Later, another storm strikes, and this time the ship goes down, repeating the cycle of the "visible Instructions" of Providence and Crusoe's "Obstinacy that nothing could resist." But this return of the storm marks a forward-moving difference, involving the greater consequence of the shipwreck, the more explicit rebuke from the shipmaster, and an enhanced sense of Crusoe's "irresistible Reluctance" to stay home. Crusoe's second ship takes him to Africa, and he engages in trade in which his 40-pound investment yields both an additional 260 pounds upon his return to London, and, he tells us, the production of "those aspiring Thoughts which have since so compleated my Ruin" (16). He then banks 200 pounds, and takes the remaining 100 with him on his next venture to Africa. However, a Turkish rover seizes this third vessel, and Crusoe becomes slave to a Moor (a kind of anticipation of Crusoe's island relationship with Friday). Crusoe again comes out of the venture with a profit, for the Portuguese captain who rescues him offers 220 pieces of eight for Xury (another anticipation of Friday), the animal hides, and the boat and its contents. The incremental accumulation of Crusoe's stock has now yielded this second economic return. Crusoe then comes ashore and uses the money to buy land for planting sugar and tobacco. He thrives until he arrives at precisely the "Middle Station" he hoped to avoid by leaving home—yet this predicament again marks a difference from the past and anticipates a forthcoming difference in his future (for on his next voyage Crusoe will indeed be cast on "some desolate Island"):

> I might as well ha' done this as well in *England* among my Friends, as ha' gone 5000 miles off to do it among Strangers and Savages in a Wilderness . . . . In this manner I used to look upon my Condition with the utmost Regret. I had no body to converse with . . . no Work to be

> done, but by the Labour of my Hands; and I used to say, I liv'd just like a Man cast away upon some desolate Island, that had no body there but himself. (30)

This entire novelistic progression indeed suggests Brooks' model of narrative, whereby repetition involves a sequentiation of temporal and material differences that delineate Crusoe's forward advance. Yet Brooks' model would tend to interpret the subject matter of Crusoe's real conditions—and the narrative mode of production by which those conditions are realized—as a textual rendering of a central—even foundational—subjective psychological formation, whereas the concept of capital would enable us to express narrative form as a self-reflexive performance of the story's economic subject matter. An economic reading, in turn, would not necessarily replace psychoanalytic tropes with economic ones, so much as bring both systems of delay, detour, and return more fully into exchange with each other at the site of fictional narrative. Put differently, this approach invites further study of the relationship between economic and psychological formations, as opposed to merely assuming the nature of that relationship. We ought not to assume so quickly, anyway, that economic identities and functions—in fiction or in economic analysis—are merely subjective psychological fabrications.

In *Beginnings: Intention and Method,* Edward Said also addresses these formal aspects of narrative delay, detour, and return, and alludes to their connection to economics without taking up mainstream analyses of capital. Said begins the chapter entitled "The Novel as Beginning Intention" with the claim that "one motive underlying the novelistic tradition in the West" involves "the desire to create an alternative world, to modify or augment the real world" (81). This interpretation of the novelistic tradition is specifically developmental:

> a central purpose of the Western novel is to enable the writer to represent characters and societies more or less freely in development . . . . Novels, therefore, are aesthetic objects that fill gaps in an incomplete world; they satisfy a human urge to add to reality . . . . the institution of narrative prose fiction [is] a kind of appetite that writers develop for modifying reality—as if from the beginning—as a desire to create a new or beginning fictional entity while accepting the consequences of that desire. (82)

Accordingly, Said's analysis is informed by a configuration of development and constraint, that tension between the power "to begin . . .

and . . . increase over what had been there previously" and the resistance to it (83). For Said, this is the predicament of both author and character. That is to say, Said reads the history of the novel in developmental terms, just as novelistic narrative is a performance of a similar production. Said's version of development in novelistic narrative calls to mind Adam Smith's account of life itself:

> the principle which prompts to save, is the desire of bettering our condition, a desire which, though generally calm and dispassionate, comes with us from the womb, and never leaves us till we go to the grave. In the whole interval which separates those two moments, there is scarce perhaps a single instant in which any man is so perfectly and completely satisfied with his situation, as to be without any wish of alteration or improvement, of any kind. (341)

Smith imagines that this story is best realized by way of economic strategies of capitalization that resemble Said's and Brooks' analyses of narrative production. Yet Said, like Brooks, does not consider the representation of capital as an analogue of his theory of narrative fiction, for his only extended reference to economic theory is Marx's *Capital* (89), whereby he reads narrative delay, detour, and return as novelistic formations of worker alienation and illusion.

In *Culture and Imperialism,* Said takes this connection between the novel and economics one step further. Arguing that "cultural forms like the novel . . . were immensely important in the formation of imperial attitudes, references, and experiences" and describing *Robinson Crusoe* as the "prototypical modern realistic novel" (xii), Said claims that Defoe's novel "inaugurated" a tradition by which the novel both reflects and actively circulates imperialist "values about contest, surmounting odds and obstacles, and patience in establishing authority through the art of *connecting principle with profit over time*" (70, my emphasis). Moreover,

> the novel is an incorporative, quasi-encyclopedic cultural form. Packed into it are both a highly regulated plot mechanism and an entire system of social reference that depends on the existing institutions of bourgeois society, their authority and power. The novelistic hero and heroine exhibit the restlessness and energy characteristic of the enterprising bourgeoisie, and they are permitted adventures in which their experiences reveal to them the limits of what they can aspire to, where they can go, what they can become. (71)

Throughout *Culture and Imperialism* Said suggests that political economy presents a variety of coincidences with novelistic narrative, except that Said makes little reference to formal classical or neoclassical economic analysis. His discussion of representations of mobility, development, and resolution in imperialist discourse, for example, could be usefully linked to formal economic analysis of free-trade, economic growth, and market equilibrium in order to explore Said's own account of the "coincidence of wants" between imperialism and the novel. On the topic of capital in particular, what Said is describing here has close ties to classical and neoclassical economic analysis in two senses: first, capital plays a role in the subject matter of the novel insofar as the genre has extensive historical, cultural, and ideological ties to capitalism; second, capital is itself theorized in economic theory in terms that resemble those aspects of novelistic form by which that subject matter is narrated. Whether we would want to explore the psychology of capital (as Brooks might) or examine how capital drives the psychology of imperialism (as Said might), capital points to a "coincidence of wants" between economics and novelistic form and content that calls for further investigation.

To which a Marxist might say yes and no. Again, to return to Crusoe's pre-island ventures, it could be argued that while capital indeed signifies a formal and thematic coincidence involving narrative and economic delay, detour, and return, those ventures also clearly depict the broader relations and exchanges of international capitalism that undercut a simple microeconomic version of the capitalizing solitary. And while Crusoe's island economy continues to tell of this coincidence, the Marxist position is that Crusoe's advance can only begin with the presence of the ship, which signifies the narrative and economic returns of those previous exchanges, expropriations, and accumulations. The problem with such a reading, however, is that it somewhat problematically must decide where the reality ends and the imagination begins—all within the confines of the fictional economy of *Robinson Crusoe*. Are Crusoe's pre-island ventures more real than the island adventure, and if so, in what sense? Why should we read the former as the mimetic key that opens the door to the ideological fiction of the latter? Are Crusoe's relations with Friday more real than his years of isolation? But if Friday is a realization of both colonialist dread and wish-fulfillment, on what grounds do we read him as the insistence of the real that ruptures the fiction of Crusoe's autonomous advance? Are the narrative incongruities and contradictions more real than its productions of coherency? While Marxist and postcolonialist critics claim that novelistic form and content are sites of capitalist ideology that suppress economic reality, how do we decide what is a suppressed formation in fiction and what is not?

For example, regarding Crusoe's capability as a producer and its relation to the production of the narrative, it is often argued (as does Hymer) that we tend to forget that Crusoe is somewhat clumsy and wasteful as a producer of capital. This would be an instance of how the fiction betrays its own ideological work. His first home caves in, his pasty pots are rather pathetic, he spends vast time and energy building a landlocked canoe, his consumption of entire trees for hewing out single wooden boards seems ridiculously inefficient, and his rise to the challenge of growing grain is not much more uplifting than the unleavened bread he bakes from it. But this critique of Crusoe's literal productivity does not detract whatsoever from the degree to which *Robinson Crusoe* is itself shaped by a path of capital formation *and* the performance of that production as narrative technique—what we might refer to as the symbolic economies of capital. Whether we read this story as an account of Crusoe's literal failure or success as a producer of capital, the narrative form and economic subject matter are mutually structured and sustained in the elaborate tensions between the present-bound linear narration of events and the temporal and structural complexities of capital formation.

Crusoe's seeds, for example, are scattered, invested, and returned to throughout the narrative in such a way as to replicate the temporal and structural delays, detours, and returns of capital. This is one crucial reason Crusoe has to keep interrupting and repeating himself, reformulating his narrative, and jumping ahead and recounting backwards—the story of capital cannot be fully produced in the present, as it structurally binds different time frames into a narrative sequence of investment and realization. The familiar question of whether Defoe's narrative is "ragged" or "artful" can be linked not only to aesthetic claims about novelistic form and its relation to "reality," or to Marxist claims about the ideological distortion of that reality, but also to capital as a site of coincidence between narrative and economic production. We can look more closely at this coincidence by examining the journal as a performance of the subjective, textual, and economic productions of *Robinson Crusoe*. For the journal presents all of those aspects of capital discussed above—the problem of beginnings, the relation between the narration of events and the production of capital, and the role of delay, detour, and return as temporal and structural configurations of that joint-production.

IV. SUNK CAPITAL AND LIQUID RETURNS

The distinction between the series of events and their narration in *Robinson Crusoe* is complicated by the presence of the journal. Indeed, it is difficult to describe the relationship between these two narrative layers or compartments found in the text—the "incomplete" journal composed on the island and Crusoe's "complete" account, which is ostensibly written after his return. In terms of chronology, for example, the production of the journal occurs before the production of the narrative return entitled *Robinson Crusoe*, and the journal therefore provides much of the "intermediate" material that yields the final production. The journal in this way resembles a kind of capital of which Crusoe makes use to produce the finished narrative. Yet the journal is not just that which comes "before" this narrative, for the journal is itself enclosed in it. This enclosure of the journal is also problematic, for the enclosure is neither temporally nor structurally contained as a distinct identity in the text; instead, the journal runs alongside the narrative, even as it increasingly gives way to that return in a roundabout fashion, much as the ink for the journal eventually runs out altogether. The journal is invested in the narrative as that which is saved and spent, and this temporal and structural transformation is itself on display. The journal yields—and yields to—novelistic returns in the sense that the journal is that which both gives way and brings forth.

We can begin exploring this relation by first noting the connection between economic and narrative production—Crusoe cannot begin writing until his economic advance has begun (e.g., the formation of capital). After bringing sufficient materials ashore from the ship and engaging in a number of capital improvements (such as the further development of his fortress enclosure and the rearrangement of his provisions), Crusoe explains that "it was a great Pleasure to me to see all my Goods in such Order, and especially to find my Stock of all Necessaries so great" (56). This realization of an improvement makes the production of narrative possible: "And now it was that I began to keep a Journal of every Day's Employment, for indeed at first I was in too much Hurry, and not only Hurry as to Labour, but in too much Discomposure of Mind, and my Journal would ha' been full of many dull things: For Example, I must have said thus. *Sept.* the 30th." Crusoe then produces an abbreviated reproduction of events already narrated—his shipwreck, his initial misery, and his plundering of the ship. But this first journalistic entry is only a hypothetical one intended to underscore how an economy of lack can only reproduce itself as a narrative analogue. Crusoe then proceeds to explain:

> But having gotten over these things in some Measure, and having settled my household Stuff and Habitation, made me a Table and a Chair, and all as handsome about me as I could, I begin to keep my Journal, of which I shall here give you the Copy (tho; in it will be told all these Particulars over again) as long as it lasted, for having no more Ink I was forc'd to leave it off. (56)

The conjunctive "But" that opens this passage is confusing, because while it marks the return to the return, as it were, in which the hypothetical journal imperceptibly gives way to the novelistic account, the transition is not really clear until the reference to the journal conveys retroactively that we have indeed returned to the account made possible by the economic improvement.

Crusoe then marks the entry of the real journal by setting off the entry with a title ("THE JOURNAL") and a dated entry ("*September 30, 1659*"). He now narrates the already twice-narrated events in different form. While the real journal makes for a more complete account than Crusoe claims would otherwise be possible, the journal is itself characterized by a lack that is later "sunk" into the production of a narrative return, hence the uncertain demarcations between these two narrative parts. For while Crusoe continues to provide dated entries, those entries are sometimes so extensive as to suggest the presence of a later narrative production. Moreover, this presence is explicitly marked by a set-off note in the entry of January 3, in which Crusoe doubles back to the earlier narrative account of fortressing his home: "This Wall being describ'd before, I purposely omit what was said in the Journal; it is sufficient to observe, that I was no less Time than from the 3d of January to the 14th of April, working, finishing, and perfecting this Wall" (61). This interruption, it should be noted, points to a coincidence between narrative form and subject matter, in which the subject of enclosure (his construction of the walls and fences) is produced as a narrative formation.

Over the next several pages Crusoe discusses his progress in a way that suggests that the journal has somehow disappeared and been replaced by the later narrative. That is, the temporal and structural markings of material events in time that signify the production of the journal (e.g., dated entries, shorter sentence structures, and narrative brevity) are absent, and it is this "going away" that produces the "return" of novelistic production. Again, this formal relation points to a connection to economic subject matter, for it is in this section that Crusoe tells of finding the bag of "Husks and Dust," scattering the seeds, and realizing their return as agricultural production. While Crusoe is "surpriz'd and perfectly astonish'd" at these "pure Productions of Providence" (63), we should also note how his own narration produces a similar economic design.

"In the Middle of all my Labours," Crusoe tells us, he discovers the grain that begins another production of delay, detour, and return (62). First, the contents of the bag constitute something of a return of his earlier voyages, for the corn is not from "This Voyage," but from the earlier trip on the Portuguese ship. Crusoe "invests" the corn by tossing it away on the ground beside his fortification. Then another short formulation of narrative delay and detour produces the return: "taking no Notice of any Thing, and not so much as remembering that I had thrown any Thing there," Crusoe is later "surpriz'd and perfectly astonish'd" when he discovers "after a little longer Time" the return of at least a little bit of England: "ten or twelve Ears . . . perfect green Barley of the same Kind as our *European*, nay, our *English* Barley" (63). In addition, some rice also shoots up, recalling for Crusoe his African exploits. International capital comes home to roost when the miraculous "pure Productions of Providence" are rendered into an economic performance of capital in Crusoe's recollection of his start-up capital of "husks and dust." Crusoe then begins his ongoing performance of capital by delaying consumption and re-routing economic resources into corn production in order to break more narrative bread later.

For just as the journal is scattered and then realized as narrative return, so too does Crusoe scatter the grain as an economic performance of "going away" that is really an investment that produces a differential return. Moreover, these economic returns are again invested in narrative production, for just as Crusoe replants the seeds, he also replicates this strategy of advance by way of delay, detour, and return in his narrative:

> But it was not till the 4th Year that I could allow my self the lest Grain of this Corn to eat, and even then but sparingly, *as I shall say afterwards in its Order*; for I lost all that I sow'd the first Season, by not observing the proper Time; for I sow'd it just before the dry Season, so that it never came up at all, at least, not as it would ha' done: *Of which in its Place*. (64, my emphasis)

This account is much like his initial description of the journal, in which formations of economic and narrative production are conjoined.

After this extended narrative delay and detour, Crusoe writes, "But to return to my Journal" (64). Yet we do not go into the journal until Crusoe returns to his own enclosure: "I work'd excessive hard these three or four Months to get my Wall done; and the 14th of April I closed it up, contriving to go into it, not by a Door, but over the Wall by a Ladder, that there might be no Sign in the Out-side of my Habitation." Crusoe then returns to the journal, as signified by the dated entry, April 16. Again, the events described there nicely suggest his problematic attempt to formulate narrative and material enclosure: "I finish'd the Ladder, so I went up with the Ladder to the Top, and then pull'd it up after me, and let it down the In-side: This was a compleat Enclosure to me." Yet just as Crusoe's journal productions are not self-contained enclosures, but are always giving away to novelistic returns, so too goes the story of Crusoe's home enclosure: "The very next Day after this Wall was finish'd, I had almost had all my Labour overthrown at once and my self kill'd, the Case was thus . . . I found the Earth come crumbling down from the Roof of my Cave" (64). Similarly, the journal again gives way to Crusoe's novelistic amplifications, and the return of the journal (April 22) is realized only when Crusoe arrives at a plan for building a new home.

In addition to the account of his wall and his corn, Crusoe's account of his parceling of the gunpowder and the enclosure of the goats (both of which suggest capitalizing strategies) is itself stored away in a narrative backtrack. "I must go back to some other Things" (49), he begins, and then narrates those experiences, after which he offers a short philosophical digression that returns him to a discussion of the powder ("as I observ'd just now"). Finally, these self-interruptions bring a promise: "I shall take it from its Beginning and continue it in its Order" (52). Nevertheless, he begins with a lapse of "ten or twelve" days that cause him to go back and mark time by putting notches on the post. Repeatedly, the temporal and structural complexities of capital are replicated in the production of their narration. The narrative footprints tracked here are not just textual or psychological formations, for they are the modes of narrative production that parallel Crusoe's strategies of economic production on the island.

At the first anniversary of his island stay, he again proposes a direct relation between the material conditions of his island economy and the production of narrative economy: "A little after this my Ink began to fail me, and so I contented my self to use it more sparingly, and to write down only the most remarkable Events of my Life, without continuing a daily *Memorandum* of other Things" (83). The journal ostensibly disappears from view. When Crusoe again takes stock of his predicament in his fourth year on the island, he writes,

> My Ink, as I observ'd had been gone some time, all but a very little, which I eek'd out with Water a little and a little, till it was so pale it scarce left any Appearance of black upon the Paper: As long as it lasted, I made use of it to minute down the Days of the Month on which any remarkable Thing happen'd to me, and first by casting up Times past: I remember that there was a strange Concurrence of Days, in the various Providences which befel me . . . . (105)

The connection between capital and narrative production is also suggestively reflected in Crusoe's supply of ink. Just as the journal is produced with the ink, the narrative return comes into production precisely because the ink is used up. The ink therefore is a representation of capital in two senses: first, it is literally a factor of production of the journal—an effect of a previous production that is itself a cause of further production; and second, its "wasting" does not just suggest the *absence* of capital production (Crusoe's ability to produce more ink), for the expenditure of the ink is a "going away" that returns as *Robinson Crusoe*. While Crusoe notes the relation between his own narrative production and the productions of Providence (a relation the ink in part makes manifest for him), this coincidence is realized in terms of the material conditions of advance largely delineated by the temporal and structural capacities of capital. Without the journal, Crusoe could still produce a narrative in which capital would appear as subject matter, but the presence of the journal—its role as an intermediate production that "yields" to the narrative return of a more complete account—puts production on display in such a way as to self-reflexively perform that subject matter.

As with the ship, critics have widely addressed the production of the journal as a link between narrative form and content, in which, for example, religious, psychological, and economic concerns function as interpretive linchpins. Generally speaking, critics read Crusoe's journalistic and narrative productions as formations that variously realize the production of something missing—an absence or a lack or an instability of some sort, such as a sense of Providential design, psychological identity, or material security. For example, Ian A. Bell makes a distinction between Crusoe as "static narrator and dynamic participant. Crusoe the wanderer is the book's source of instability; Crusoe the narrator its source of stability" (160). Similarly, Robert A. Erickson makes a connection between the 17th- and 18th-century "literature of generation" and Crusoe's attempts to produce his own birth on the island. Erickson reads Crusoe's propensities for building enclosures (cages, traps, pens, pitfalls, forts) as a desire to create beginning points that resemble maternal spaces, and argues that these attempts to take possession of the island parallel his attempt to take possession of himself. Homer O. Brown takes this relation one step further, by examining the relationship between these enclosures, Crusoe's various displacements of self, and *Robinson Crusoe*'s textual formations. Brown notes how pervasively patterns of concealment and exposure shape the narrative, as in Crusoe's fear of engulfment by a range of threats (such as storms and cannibals). Brown links this pattern to Crusoe's unstable subjectivity and his attempts to achieve stability between himself and the world, as well as between his experience and his narrative productions of that experience. Brown argues that "Crusoe's journal . . . represents an attempt to give the shifting moments of a subjective time something like the spatial ordering in the same way that he carves notches into a post" (584-5). Brown also notes Crusoe's various productions of beginnings, which he links to the journal and its various gaps, discrepancies, and repetitions. Michael McKeon attempts to link soteriological and psychological concerns as a kind of joint-production realized in the complexities of the journal and the narrative.

Other critics have explored the journal as a textual performance that more pointedly suggests a relation between narration and capital formation. Mary E. Butler, for example, argues that the journal puts production on display. She inventories not only the larger structural discrepancies noted by critics like Brown, but also the more local stylistic uncertainties of Crusoe's syntax that underscore a fundamental incommensurability between his experience and its reproduction in writing. She offers an excellent inventory of Crusoe's syntactic tendency for double-entry, rupture, and backtracking. These include compound constructions of words, phrases, and entire clauses in which elaboration and contradiction suggest a pattern of uncertainty, a compulsion for repetition and transformation, and the inexpressible and ineffable nature of experience whose narrative reproduction is never finished. Accordingly, Butler argues that the "subject of *Robinson Crusoe* is the process of making."

In "Crusoe's Legacy," Richard Braverman makes an argument for reading Crusoe's familial disobedience and island adventure in terms of the political and philosophical conflict between the authority of the sovereign and the rights of men of property, which he links to both writing and capital. Braverman's claim is that Defoe is invoking a Lockean theory of labor and property to trace Crusoe's journey from obedient son to autonomous "father," a familial narrative with political and economic parallels in emerging capitalist society. Although Braverman's focus on the links between economics and narrative primarily involves labor and language, capital nevertheless circulates as a central figure. Braverman claims that from the ship "Crusoe principally retrieves the instruments of empirical, technical knowledge, tools emblematic of human reason that are the symbolic instruments of power in the post-patriarchialist order of capital relations" (9). Braverman writes that "the initial problem of scarcity eventually becomes a problem of surplus because [of] his intervention into the 'natural' reproductive order" (11), and capital accumulation is the primary signifier of this labor, for

> that surplus, like his knowledge, is an aspect of accumulation which is at the foundation of his 'capital' sovereignty. In effect, Crusoe redeems himself through the labor of husbanding and the economy of accumulation or investment—the capitalization of the body politic. (12)

Braverman suggests that this allegory of political transition (from the innate claims of the sovereign to the labored property of the capitalist) is similarly realized in the novel's presentation of linguistic instrumentalism, which Braverman explores primarily in terms of the journal. The journal, in turn, is closely tied to capital accumulation:

> words are instruments—capital, or 'ingenious labor' . . . . Crusoe represents the systemic revision through an analogy of words as the tools or instruments of knowledge in the island's productive and political economies. The instrumental order of the word is established through the relation between Crusoe's journal . . . and the tools that he brings to shore from the ship. The new relationship between word and tool is illustrated by the fundamental problem of ordering that occurs after Crusoe salvages all the goods he can from the ship but before he begins to record his adventures in the journal. (13)

Braverman notes that only after Crusoe organizes his "confused" heap into a functioning "warehouse" does the self-representation of the journal begin. But for Braverman, labor is the key to material and literary (re)production. That is, while he points to the role of capital, he takes the Marxist approach (via Locke) and "reads through" the instrumentality of capital in order to interpret narrative as a performance of labor.

In a similar move, Peter Hulme argues that the production of the journal bears on what he calls the "secret of capital" in the novel. Hulme argues that economic and spiritual readings have as a common concern the question of *plot*—how the "formal realism" of the novel negotiates the tension of producing both a "coherent narrative" and the "texture of daily experience" (178). Whereas spiritual readings attempted to "remedy the scandal" (179) of the formal incoherencies of the episodic secular text described by critics such as Watt, Hulme argues that "the realistic *detail* of the text obscures elements of the narrative that . . . would have to be called . . . the primary stuff of colonialist ideology" (186). Rejecting both spiritual readings and "facile versions of the relationship between the fictional and the politico-economic discourses of the eighteenth century" (187), Hulme argues that the narrative coherency and the "radical textual disturbance" in *Robinson Crusoe* have "ideological implications for colonialist discourse" (193).

Hulme traces these implications in terms of the connection between the "beginning moment that [colonialist] discourse hesitates over" and the "desperate difficulties the text has in composing Crusoe's self, an activity, as the word indicates, every bit as much scriptive as it is psychological" (193). Both Crusoe's production of himself and the production of *Robinson Crusoe* are performances of colonial desire and dread—how the colonialist wants to imagine himself, the threats to that identity, and the attempt to arrive at stability and mastery. For Hulme the narrative technique of *Robinson Crusoe* is the fictional instrument that produces the capitalist "alibi" for the colonial exploitation of labor. Hulme's exploration of the "radical textual disturbance" in the novel calls attention to those "fictions of wholeness" constituting Crusoe's psychological subjectivity, the narrative economy of *Robinson Crusoe*, and the "colonial romance" performed there. For example, Hulme notes the pattern of dreams and wish-fulfillment in the novel, "those complex moments of replication . . . where the narrative seems to fold over on to itself in a way disturbingly unlike any realistic transcription of the empirically real" (204). Following this line, Hulme goes on to explore the "extraordinary sequence of benefactors that Crusoe relies on" and describes this sequence as "an aspect of that ideologeme of 'wish-fulfillment' identified by [Northrop] Frye as central to the romance form." Moreover, Hulme argues that this benevolence is a "*narrative* device which holds together the many disparate strands of Crusoe's commercial activity" (212-3). As examples, he cites the captain on Crusoe's first adventure, the captain's widow, the Portuguese captain, various English merchants, and his Brazilian plantation partner and trustees. This romance configuration produces the colonial subjectivity that is "simultaneously an individual and a national consciousness, both forged in the smithy of [the] Caribbean," a narrative formation of dreams, benevolence, and wish-fulfillment involving "mastering . . . trauma through repetition" of events both real and imagined in the fiction (216-7).

Yet the result of Hulme's approach is to "read through" precisely the productive instrumentality that he himself argues has produced the fiction. Hulme's description of Crusoe's store of narrative techniques (the production of the journal, dreams and wish-fulfillment, repetition and transformation, and structural displacement) is fundamentally analogous to the configuration of delay, detour, and return by which classical and neoclassical economics represent capital. But Hulme's reading ultimately dismisses this mode of production as "mere fiction" in order to arrive at the very sort of Marxist mimetic allegory he claims to eschew. So, whereas Hulme tends to read these formations as colonial romance alibi, I have argued that these formations of delay, detour, and return are themselves self-reflexive productions of how capital actually works in *Robinson Crusoe*.

Hulme argues that the delay and detour of Crusoe's realization of his Brazilian plantation, which for Hulme represents the historical and economic reality of colonialism that *Robinson Crusoe* marginalizes and suppresses, finally arrives at the return of a kind of spectral truth. Hulme points to how much trouble the narrative has in reconciling the imaginary economy of the island with the reality of colonial slave labor, a fictional production of repression and displacement whose revelation at the end of his island enterprise temporarily overwhelms Crusoe, whose discovery of his wealth upon his return "marks the discovery of the secret of capital itself, that it accumulates in magical independence from the labour of its owner" (220). But for Hulme, the "magical independence" of capital refers not to the instrumentality of capital as a factor of production distinct from labor in *Robinson Crusoe*, but to the suppression of the exploitation of labor elsewhere:

> The imperial production of *Robinson Crusoe* . . . foregrounds the colonial alibi . . . . and the book's tremendous effort to reconstruct that economy fills up the narrative space in which, in that other place, silently, Crusoe's other self, his ghostly "partner", is developing those plantations on the violently-extracted labour-power of slaves which will provide the capital to displace that moral economy with a less volatile mode of production. (222)

Hulme, then, also reads narrative technique as a performance of capital. However, he reads this "imperial production" as fictional alibi, whereas I propose that the narrative production of capital directs our attention to somewhere else than the scene of some historical crime. The paradox here is that Hulme engages in a similar "tremendous effort" of reconstructing a moral economy in order to "fill up the narrative space" of *Robinson Crusoe*, for it is there that we are to discover the secret of *labor* as the "ghostly partner" in this fiction of capital. Yet even if we wish to see labor as the source of all value, or slave labor as the secret of colonial economic advance, we also remember that capital makes certain modes of production possible. For as Hulme acknowledges, it is still somehow the instrument of *capital* that gets the job done and the story told.

NOTES

[1] This aspect of the story is brought into suggestive relief by comparing it with J. M. Coetzee's *Foe*, a fictional revision in which the "real" Crusoe engages in almost none of this capital formation. This Crusoe, in turn, has nothing to say. This economic lack and narrative silence is observed first-hand by a woman who is herself shipwrecked on the island, spends a year there with Crusoe and Friday, returns to England, and tells her story to "Mr. Foe," who then formulates a much different story. Coetzee adds a nice touch by remarking the absence of a journal, thereby underscoring the connection between narration and capital formation.

[2] Qtd. in Shinagel, 283.

[3] Qtd. in Shinagel, 291.

[4] The connections among these versions of Crusoe are also interesting. For example, Campe's version was the source of reference for the nineteenth-century German economist H. H. Gossen, who anticipated elements of neoclassical microeconomic utility theory, and who used Crusoe as a model in his analysis.

[5] Perhaps it is no more accurate to say that Crusoe anticipates neoclassical models than it is to claim that marginal utility analysis begins with the neoclassical economists in the latter part of the nineteenth-century. Indeed, one can find evidence of aspects of utility theory in pre-classical and classical political economy (e.g., Bernoulli and Galiani).

[6] Qtd. in Shinagel, 296.

[7] Not only are these two works often cited as having something like originary positions in histories of the modern novel and political economy respectively, but we can find much of Defoe's economic sensibilities anticipated in Smith's work. Smith's work represents an important synthesis of many of the concepts and arguments with which Defoe was both familiar and actively involved as a political writer, hired hack, and businessman. While Defoe was not

very important as an innovative economic thinker, he was throughout his life deeply concerned with economic matters (especially the subject of "trade," which circulates as a kind of totem in his prose) and he was perhaps the most significant and prolific economic journalist of his time. Both Richetti and Novak offer succinct discussions of Defoe's political and economic writing. His more familiar economic writings include *An Essay upon Projects* (1697), *The Villainy of Stock-Jobbers Detected* (1701), his articles in *Review* (1704-1713) and *Mercator* (1713-1714), *A General History of Trade* (1713), *An Essay on Ways and Mans for the Advancement of Trade* (1726), *The Complete English Tradesman* (1727), and *A Brief State of the Inland or Home Trade, of England* (1730).

[8] For an economist's critical perspective of the relationship between nineteenth-century physics and neoclassical economics, see Philip Mirowski, *More Heat than Light: Economics as Social Physics: Physics as Nature's Economics.*

CHAPTER 3

Entrepreneurial Recombinations in *Frankenstein*

. . . a dream has power to poison sleep.
We rise; one wandr'ing thought pollutes
the day.

—PERCY SHELLEY, "MUTABILITY"

In Mary Shelley's *Frankenstein*, Victor Frankenstein wonders, why the waste of death? This is really a two-part question that also bears its own answer, for his challenge to death brings forth his attempt to produce life from it, as he recombines human remains in an innovative enterprise that he believes will benefit mankind. What we might describe as Victor's attempt to recycle garbage by putting parts of dead bodies back into circulation in society suggests that he is not just a scientist, a romantic artist, a criminal, or a parent, which are several of the more familiar roles in which critics have variously cast him.[1] Instead, I wish to argue three related points. First, Victor also resembles the innovative, risk-taking economic agent, or entrepreneur, who creatively recombines the factors of his production in order to bring forth a new kind of enterprise for the benefit of himself and society. Second, a close examination of the similarities between Shelley's gothic rendering of enterprise and the depiction of the entrepreneur in mainstream classical and neoclassical economic discourse enables us to see more fully both the economic content of the book and its relation to those "non-economic" aspects of this novel that are typically associated with romantic notions of individual identity and agency, creativity and risk, personal privacy and revelation, and social triumph and failure. Finally, this coincidence between literary and economic figuration raises compelling questions about the relationship between novelistic fiction and capitalism more broadly, such as how literary and economic texts might variously anticipate, reflect, and amplify one another.

We can begin to examine this entrepreneurial economy in Shelley's novel by first paying some attention to words. Throughout *Frankenstein*, we encounter many references to "enterprise" and "undertaking." Walton repeatedly refers to his polar expedition as a "great enterprise" (15, 17, 27); Victor likewise discusses his project as an "undertaking" (53) that would realize his youthful dreams of "great enterprise" (203), much as he refers to Walton's as a similarly "honourable undertaking" (207); Clerval looks to the Oriental East as "affording scope for his spirit of enterprise"(67); and at the end Victor exhorts Walton (rather ambiguously, as we shall see) to "undertake my unfinished work" (209).

These similar instantiations of enterprise and undertaking among the main characters point to a suggestive coincidence with economic representations of the entrepreneur. For it is useful to remember that until late in the nineteenth century, English political economists used only the word "undertaker" to refer to the entrepreneurial agent.[2] At the same time, "undertaker" also had other usages, such as the one who makes a business of carrying out arrangements for funerals. To be sure, the word has had a range of meanings that preclude a determined link solely with economic enterprise. Even so, the history of its usage in relation to both the "dismal science" and the business of death-dealing offers a framework for exploring the ambivalent and ambiguous depiction of Victor's charnal dealings in life and death in relation to the economic representation of the entrepreneur who, somewhat analogously, is cast as an agent of both personal and social creativity and destruction.

Although previous interpretations of *Frankenstein* have also argued for reading Victor and his undertaking in economic terms, they tend to proceed from a Marxist account of the central conflict between capital and labor, a version in which the roles of the capitalist and the entrepreneur are conflated.[3] In most readings Victor is assigned the position of capitalist, while the distinct role of the entrepreneur is altogether overlooked, as if he were an unrecognizable confabulation in both gothic and capitalist fictions. In classical and neoclassical economic analysis, however, the entrepreneur gradually emerges as an identity or a function in production which is distinct from that of the capitalist. The capitalist merely owns capital and makes it available to others, whereas it is the entrepreneur who recombines and animates all of the factors of production (land, labor, and capital) into innovative formulations that disturb the equilibrium of the marketplace. The entrepreneur is the one whose creativity and risk-taking is rewarded with profit, which is distinct from the interest, wages, and rent that accrue to the capitalist, laborer, and landowner respectively. At the same time, this version of the romantic entrepreneurial quest places its economic hero in a kind of ironic or tragic narrative of inevitable failure, whereby the market either fails to recognize the entrepreneurial contribution or appropriates it altogether. In the most basic free-market scenario, either the entrepreneurial innovation fails to gain acceptance or it is eventually absorbed by the expiration of entrepreneurial protections (such as monopolies and patents) and the competitive elimination of the market "friction" economists refer to as profits. Market equilibrium, as it were, returns the entrepreneurial difference to zero.

Entrepreneurial animation and disturbance can be detected in a number of sites of "enterprise" in Shelley's fiction. Indeed, Victor, Walton, and Clerval are all men of ambitious pursuits who would seem to present a clear distinction between economic enterprise and their own respective undertakings, as each of them explicitly rejects an interest in business concerns and the attainment of wealth. Yet what they ostensibly dread presents a number of connections with what they manifestly desire, insofar as their sensibilities and actions are intricately tied to entrepreneurial figurations of individual creativity, risk, and their ability to effect a beneficial material change in the society. This relation between economic enterprise and their various undertakings is neither strictly literal nor entirely metaphorical, for while an explicit economic content is repeatedly suggested (as in Walton's desire for new trade routes and Clerval's colonialist ambitions), this material is portrayed (by Shelley and her readers) as little more than a kind of reconstituted body part stitched into Shelley's gothic rendering of that which is both more marvelous and more horrible than the banalities of the marketplace.

So the economic pieces are there, even if not quite as previous economic readings would have them. For interpretations that fail to recognize the entrepreneur cannot adequately articulate Victor's enterprise or Shelley's. For example, Victor is neither just an owner of capital, nor a laborer who finds himself in a workshop in which the factors of production are already in place. He also animates all of the factors of production in a creative and risk-taking enterprise that disturbs the material conditions and social conventions of what is familiar, natural, and even possible. He does not just own the modes of production that make monster-making possible, nor is he employed on the workshop floor making monsters out of the predetermined parts that come his way. Shelley's narrative, accordingly, is not a rendition of capitalist exploitation and/or worker alienation, but a version of entrepreneurial creativity, risk, and innovation, in which the anticipation and realization of uncertain personal profit and loss is similarly played out in the dialectic of creative destruction and productive change in the social sphere.

This relation between economic figuration and literary formation is indeed an ambiguous production ambivalently rendered, for just as these charges of the marvelous and the horrible are conducted in Victor's "workshop of filthy creation" and in Shelley's gothic mode of fiction, so too are they grounded in the economic version of the entrepreneur, which I explore in the next section.

II. ENTREPRENEURS LOST AND FOUND

A brief overview of the representation of the entrepreneur in classical and neoclassical analysis (as well as mention of those economic readings of *Frankenstein* that can find no such entrepreneurial appearance there) requires that two qualifying points be kept in view: First, as noted above, although a distinction is made between the capitalist and the entrepreneur, it is not always a clear one. The relation between them is somewhat problematic, as in, for example, the differentiation between entrepreneurial identity and function, as well as in the designation of the economic returns that accrue to the capitalist and the entrepreneur respectively. Second, the articulation of the entrepreneur is gradually realized in the history of economic thought, in the sense that while he indeed is present in earlier pre-classical and classical analysis, he emerges more explicitly in later neoclassical analysis. In other words, just as the romantic hero flickers into existence upon the tableau of Shelley's novel, so too is this economic hero only slowly and somewhat inconsistently recognized as a distinct economic identity in the history of modern mainstream political economy.

The economic usage of the term "entrepreneur" (from the French *entreprendre*, or "to embark or to undertake") is conventionally traced back to Richard Cantillon's *Essai sur la nature du commerce en general* (1755). Cantillon was a pre-classical thinker whose innovative work anticipates much of the classical approach that formally begins with Adam Smith's *Wealth of Nations* (1776). Cantillon made important contributions to the conception of the economy as a sort of Newtonian system of interconnected forces that tend toward equilibrium, and his analysis addressed adjustment mechanisms involving population, supply and demand, market prices, monetary velocity, and international trade. Vital to this system is the role of the self-interested entrepreneur. In Cantillon's view, the entrepreneur essentially operates as a risk-taker who makes certain choices in the present in order to realize uncertain results in the future. Cantillon organizes the economy into classes of individuals defined by their economic function:

> We may conclude that, with the exception of the Prince and the Proprietors of Lands, all the Inhabitants . . . may be divided into two classes, namely, Entrepreneurs and Wage-Earners; and that the Entrepreneurs work for uncertain wages, so to speak, and all others for certain wages until they have them, although their functions and ranks are very disproportionate. The General who has his salary, the Courtier who has a pension, and the Domestic who has wages, are in the latter class. All the others are Entrepreneurs, whether they establish themselves with a capital to carry on their own enterprise, or are Entrepreneurs of their own work without any capital, and they may be considered as living subject to uncertainty; even Beggars and Robbers are Entrepreneurs of this class. (54)

As early as Cantillon, then, some distinction is made between the identity or function of the capitalist and that of the entrepreneur. Victor Frankenstein resembles this entrepreneurial position in a number of ways. First; he is a kind of speculator who sees what others do not yet see, and then reproduces that vision as a material and social reality. Second, this innovative enterprise involves an element of uncertainty or risk, in which the entrepreneur's attempt to close the gap between the real and the unreal has unforeseeable consequences. Third, Victor is both an entrepreneur who has capital (e.g., access to the modes of production) and one who procures it from others (most notably in his use of body parts). Finally, both Cantillon's market economy and Shelley's gothic narrative similarly require the freedom and mobility of agents and resources as the condition that makes possible what Cantillon refers to as "all the exchange and circulation," even as this process also brings with it constant uncertainty and threat of failure (70).

Cantillon was more influential in France (as in the work of J. B. Say) than in England, and it was not until 1881 that Cantillon's importance was "rediscovered" (if perhaps overstated) by the English neoclassical economist William Stanley Jevons, who called the *Essai* "the cradle of political economy."[4] In the meantime, however, British classical analysis reflects a growing awareness of the entrepreneur, even if the articulation of his identity and function is somewhat inconsistent and only variously realized. Classical economists tended to speak of the factors of production in terms of landowner, capitalist, and laborer, whose contributions are returned, respectively, as rent, profit, and wages.[5] As mentioned earlier, these economists generally saw the capitalist and the entrepreneur as a single agent who goes by a different name in English—the "undertaker." (Although the word "entrepreneur" appears in English early in the nineteenth century, as in reference to one who "gets up" musical performances, it does not circulate widely in economic discourse until the twentieth century.) In *Wealth of Nations*, for example, Adam Smith speaks of "the undertaker of the work who hazards his stock in this adventure," and whose "profits should bear a regular proportion to his capital" (66-7). We can see in this formulation no explicit or stable distinction between the one who possesses capital and the one who undertakes to put that capital into innovative and risky modes of production—or between the rewards that accrue to those respective functions. Yet Smith does point to a distinction in his attempt to delineate the relation between the price of a good and the income accruing to each of the owners of the factors of its production:

> Whoever derives his revenue from a fund which is his own, must draw it either from his labour, from his stock, or from his land. The revenue derived from his labour is called wages. That derived from stock, by the person who manages or employs it, is called profit. That derived from it by the person who does not employ it himself, but lends it to another, is called the interest or use of money. It is the compensation which the borrower pays to the lender, for the profit which he has an opportunity of making by the use of the money. Part of the profit naturally belongs to the borrower who runs the risk and takes the trouble of employing it; and part to the lender, who affords him the opportunity. . . . The revenue which proceeds altogether from land, is called rent. (69-70)

Smith goes on to note, "When those different sorts of revenue belong to different persons, they are readily distinguished; but when they belong to the same they are sometimes confounded with one another, at least in common language" (70). Yet we might note that they continue to be confounded in economic analysis as well, for this uncertain distinction involving the role of "running the risk" and "taking the trouble," as well as the relation between interest and profit as the returns of two different economic functions, continues throughout nineteenth-century British political economy. For example, the British classical economist John Stuart Mill makes reference to this distinction in *Principles of Political*

Economy (1848): "The difference between the interest and the gross profit remunerates the exertions and risks of the undertaker" (479). This distinction, moreover, is also implicit in French classical analysis, such as that of the economist J. B. Say, which, reflecting Cantillon's influence on French political economy, describes the entrepreneurial function as combining the factors of production. (His notion of entrepreneurial "combination," incidentally, nicely suggests Victor's recombination of dead body parts.)

In neoclassical analysis toward the end of the century, this ambiguity is reflected in discussions of entrepreneurial "combination" and "direction," which often suggest only simple business management, superintendence, or administration. Yet nineteenth-century economists did give increasing attention to the entrepreneur as risk-taker and innovator, and they presented a variety of distinctions between entrepreneurial profits and the reward of interest to capital. The neoclassical economist Alfred Marshall, for example, writes in his *Principles of Economics* (1890) that

> the task of so directing production . . . has to be broken up and given into the hands of a specialized body of . . . business men. They 'adventure' or 'undertake' its risks; they bring together capital and labour required for the work; they arrange or 'engineer' its general plan, and superintend its minor details. (293)

Marshall makes distinctions between "undertakers" who risk capital and actual manufacturers who are the employers of labor; he observes "the relations in which the undertaking of risks stands to the rest of the work of the business man" (293); he argues for "the truth that the superintendence of labour is but one side, and often not the most important side of business work"; he claims that "the employer who undertakes the whole risks of his business really performs two entirely distinct services" (297); and he "divide[s] employers and other undertakers into two classes, those who open out new and improved methods of business, and those who follow beaten tracks" (597). Nevertheless, his discussion of the entrepreneur is largely subsumed under the notion of "business management," which tends to conflate capitalist and entrepreneurial functions, as is reflected in somewhat unclear distinctions between the "price of business ability and energy" and the "price of that organization by which business ability and the requisite capital are brought together" (313).

Perhaps the strongest and most vivid articulation of the entrepreneur can be found in the work of the twentieth-century economist Joseph Schumpeter, whose notion of the "creative destruction" of capitalist development focused on the entrepreneur as the key agent who disturbs the "natural state" of the marketplace by introducing change and disequilibrium.[6] For Schumpeter, the entrepreneur represents a specific economic function different from that of the landowner, capitalist, and laborer. The entrepreneurial agent may or may not be a capitalist, but the entrepreneurial *function* is distinct insofar as it entails the innovation of new combinations of the elements of economic production. As Cantillon had argued, the entrepreneur need not be connected with the possession of wealth, nor should he be equated solely with the management or superintendence of an ongoing operation. While the entrepreneurial function is, as Smith reminds us, often commingled with other functions, it nevertheless signifies a distinct place in the economy in its realization of "new combinations" in production, and therefore both the destruction of the old conditions and the formation of the new. Whether working within or extending the frame of a given technological horizon, improvising new methods of production, creating new goods or improving old ones, or developing new consumer markets, the entrepreneur imagines and then realizes that which has not been done before in the economic marketplace. At the same time, this version of economic advance also suggests a model of the market as a dynamic system of forces always tending toward equilibrium, for although the entrepreneur introduces a force or difference that disrupts and destabilizes the equilibrium of the system, this entrepreneurial injection is itself eventually dissipated or neutralized, as technological and legal monopolies give way, innovation becomes routine, and profits approach zero. This is, as it were, a romantic narrative of economic creation and destruction in a market system whose dynamics constitute a kind of dialectic between entrepreneurial instability and systemic equilibrium.

As will be discussed at more length in the next section, Victor resembles this creative and risk-taking entrepreneur who combines the factors of production in an innovative enterprise that disrupts the natural state of things. He is the individual who both utilizes the existing technological horizon and furthers it, he attempts to recombine and animate resources of production into a new configuration that threatens the status quo with "creative destruction," he encounters the problem of entrepreneurial control and ownership of that innovation, and he is himself doomed to inevitable failure or dissolution, whether we read the fate of his undertaking as that which is either literally rejected by, or symbolically integrated into, the gothic economy in which it is produced.

Literary analysis of economic concerns in *Frankenstein* is generally informed by Marxist theory, which is, of course, less interested in the entrepreneur than is classical and neoclassical market analysis, with its emphasis on individual creativity and risk as genuine factors of economic production. Like Marxist theory, these critical readings focus on the conditions and contributions of capital and labor, as well as the central class conflict between them. Marxist critics discuss Victor as the alienated factory worker in his "workshop of filthy creation" or as the bourgeois capitalist horrified by the proletariat monster. Similarly, they often read the monster as labor (denoting the dehumanization of the worker) or as capital itself (the animated reification of technology).

Yet previous readings, regardless of their various seating assignments, can find no place for the entrepreneur as a distinct economic figure. A good example of this can be found in Elsie B. Michie's "*Frankenstein* and Marx's Theories of Alienated Labor," in which she argues that while "Shelley's novel contains no explicit depictions of workers, the marketplace, or the forces of production," Fredric Jameson's notion of the "political unconscious" enables one to find an economic symbolic there. [7] While noting that the monster can be read as a representation of the alienated worker, she argues that Victor, too, stands in as a figure of labor:

> This new reading seems contradictory because the novel clearly represents Victor as coming from the upper, moneyed classes. The problem here is that we are moving from the easy one-to-one correspondence of a strictly allegorical reading, which sees Victor as *entrepreneur* and the Creature as a worker, to a symbolic reading, which sees issues of production represented at various locations throughout the novel. (94, my emphasis)

Michie's resistance to "easy" Marxist allegory and her deployment of Jameson's notion of narrative as a symbolic site of the "political unconscious" together offer a compelling reading of novelistic form and content as economic configurations. Nevertheless, note how she revises the "easy" formulation of Victor by way of a conflation of capitalist and entrepreneur. In this way, Michie can reduce the narrative to a binary equation of capital and labor, reverse their respective positions within this symbolic economy, and then "replace stories of creation with accounts of production" (97). However, *Frankenstein* is about innovative and uncertain creativity *and* its realization as production, and an economic reading need not resist or repress the former in order to engage the latter. The concept of the entrepreneur enables us to remember that Victor's workshop is not a site of an already determined and strictly mechanistic production; instead, it is a representation of the creative animation of that site of production, as well as the disturbances this creativity produces.

Similarly, Warren Montag argues (in "'The Workshop of Filthy Creation': A Marxist Reading of *Frankenstein*") that the novel can be read as a gothic displacement and repression of the economic and political conditions that Shelley ambivalently regarded in early nineteenth-century Europe. Citing the lack of scientific and technological detail, as well as the absence of an urban landscape in the romantic representations of nature, Montag traces how the novel suggests an economic discourse (e.g., Victor's "workshop" as a site of industrial activity) while suppressing that discourse in favor of the "immateriality of creation." In other words, "the text itself turns with loathing from the images that it produces" (309). However, because the entrepreneur—as an identity or function distinct from that of the capitalist—has no recognizable place within the Marxist economy, Montag, too, "turns with loathing" from this particular economic agent and function. Finally, this move generates a somewhat ironic reification of a gap between economic and non-economic spheres, insofar as this is a Marxist reading that would seek to conjoin economic and literary production by insisting on a mutually exclusive relation between material production and "immaterial creation," in which the representation of the latter suppresses the reality of the former.

This inability to recognize the figuration of the entrepreneur in Shelley's novel presents two sorts of problems, one involving reading this particular text, and the other involving how this reading might influence (and be influenced by) theoretical considerations of the relationship between literary and economic discourse more broadly. First, in reducing Victor's workshop to the site of economic production involving only capital and labor, these readings do not satisfactorily address those elements of uncertainty, risk, creativity, and innovation that crucially shape Victor's subjective states, his mode of production, his social relations, and their material consequences. The Marxist framework precludes us from recognizing the way in which the entrepreneurial and gothic animation and disturbance give chase, as it were, to one another. Second, if Marxist interpretations were to recognize this entrepreneurial coincidence between economic and literary formations, they would subject those formations to an ideological critique that would recognize them only as a sort of joint-production of false-consciousness, in which bourgeois economics and romantic gothic conspire to deny real economic conditions. Yet even if we were to critique the economic entrepreneur as a sort of ideological fabrication (or if we were to theorize gothic fiction in the same way), we could more productively do so by paying closer attention to how that entrepreneurial fiction might operate in Shelley's novel, and then go on to elaborate a more comprehensive account of the machinations of the "political unconscious" at either economic or literary sites of production. At the same time, if this "coincidence of wants" between economic and literary production makes its appearance only through the borrowed lens of a non-Marxist perspective, we ought not to cast a blind eye to the question of just how useful the Marxist models are for reading this literary work. Perhaps an inability to recognize the entrepreneur as an economic identity might replicate itself as a failure to grasp the mode of his production as a literary formation.

III. THE ENTREPRENEURIAL ECONOMY OF *FRANKENSTEIN*

Economics functions as an explicit element of a number of subplots in *Frankenstein*. For example, Beaufort, a friend of Victor's father, is a merchant who falls from a "flourishing state" into poverty (31), an economic decline that ultimately results in the marriage of Beaufort's daughter Catherine to Victor's father Alphonse, a union which, of course, produces Victor. (Moreover, Beaufort's retreat from Geneva to Lucerne and Alphonse Frankenstein's search for him also suggests the pervasive pattern of mobility and pursuit in the novel that I discuss below.) These economic inflections of plot are replicated in the De Lacey story, in which Safie's father, like Beaufort, is a merchant whose loss of wealth and ensuing movements result in a daughter functioning as object of desire and exchange (119-123). Similar economic mobility also informs Elizabeth's and Justine's entries into the Frankenstein family. In each of these subplots, the melodrama of mobility is scripted by economic conditions.

The entrepreneurial sensibilities of Walton, Clerval, and Victor are similarly tied to a challenge to the patriarchal status quo, in which in each instance the son seeks to disrupt both familial and social equilibria by introducing new enterprises resisted by the father. This pattern figuratively and literally suggests the emergence of a new capitalist system of market identities and relations, economic growth and social mobility, and the development of an international economy. For example, the novel opens with Walton's letter to his sister in which he refers to his father's "dying injunction" that forbade him "to embark in a seafaring life" (14). Walton has disobeyed his father, and writes his sister en route to tell her of his successful "commencement of an enterprise" to find a more direct passage to the North Pole and to "discover the wondrous power which attracts the needle" (14). Walton's story commences by way of this entrepreneurial spirit, even if the quest is not strictly economic in emphasis. Walton notes that "my life might have been passed in ease and luxury; but I preferred glory to every enticement that wealth placed in my path" (15). However, economics literally underwrites both his venture and its production as narrative: Walton's travels are made possible by his inheritance of a cousin's fortune, he learns his skills as a sailor by way of the whaling industry, his curiosity about a passage to the North is linked to establishing new international trade routes, and merchants literally transport at least part of the correspondence between Walton and his sister, who remains in England. Walton's enterprise is linked to the emergence of market capitalism, as well as to a specific cultural history of English imperialism.

Even more than Walton, Clerval's conflict with his father specifically involves a complex blend of disengagement from and attachment to business concerns. Just as Frankenstein claims that "[w]ealth was an inferior object" (39), Clerval sees his father as "a narrow-minded trader" who cannot appreciate his son's "firm resolve . . . not to be chained to the miserable details of commerce" (43-4). However, this resistance to patriarchal pressure in *Frankenstein* suggests not so much a rejection of the marketplace as it does a challenge to a particular formulation of economic identity and agency, marking the emergence of a new entrepreneurial system. For instance, Clerval makes sarcastic jokes that would seem to enforce a clear distinction between economic concerns and his own intellectual pursuits, such as when he mocks his father's attitude about business and intellectual enterprise: "I have ten thousand florins a year without Greek, I eat heartily without Greek" (59). Yet Clerval's ambitions are themselves ultimately economic. Resolving "to pursue no inglorious career, he turned his eyes towards the East as affording scope for his spirit of enterprise." Although Clerval's Orientalism at first appears purely intellectual, for both Clerval and Frankenstein this academic "consolation in the works of the Orientalists" functions as a means toward some other material end (67). Just as this Orientalist pleasure can temporarily distract Frankenstein from his own "workshop of filthy creation" and "unwholesome toil," so too does it underwrite Clerval's economic ambitions regarding colonial trade: "He was also pursuing an object he had long had in view. His design was to visit India, in the belief that he had in his knowledge of its various languages, and in the views he had taken of its society, the means of materially assisting the progress of European colonisation and trade" (153). Again, resistance to paternal conservatism is not only metaphorically analogous to the entrepreneurial spirit, but is also literally linked to economic conditions and concerns.

Indeed, the novel repeatedly suggests various connections between economic conditions and characters' predicaments and aspirations. For example, Frankenstein's "unwholesome trade" reminds him of a condition in which he is "rather [more] like one doomed by slavery to toil in the mines . . . than an artist occupied by his favourite employment," thereby suggesting that the realms of art and science are also increasingly linked to economic contexts (55). Similarly, when Frankenstein speaks of his sense of the alienation and disequilibrium that his pursuit has brought upon him, he poses it as a rupture linked to a much broader history of slavery, imperialism, and colonial discovery. For at one point Victor claims that any "pursuit of knowledge" is both the cause and effect of a "passion or a transitory desire" that disturbs not only the "calm and peaceful mind" of the individual, but also the familial equilibrium, both of which ultimately lead to a kind of restlessness signified by the social disruption and economic exploitation:

> if no man allowed any pursuit whatsoever to interfere with the tranquillity of domestic affections, Greece had not been enslaved; Caesar would have spared his country; America would have been discovered more gradually; and the empires of Mexico and Peru had not been destroyed. (54)

In the monster's narrative we also encounter similar figurations of an economic content. The monster is himself a productive technology or personification of industrialism that changes the rural De Lacy household by attempting to "assist their labours" (108). The monster also echoes Adam Smith's notion of the market mechanism by which society's needs are satisfied when he describes himself as the "invisible hand" (112) that supplies the De Lacy household with a variety of goods and services. Finally, the monster learns about the economies of colonialism and class conflict when he reads of the "hapless fate" of American Indians and "the division of property, of immense wealth and squalid poverty," a predicament he attempts to bring to bear on his own identity: "The words induced me to turn toward myself. . . . And what was I?" The monster proceeds to link this history of economic disenfranchisement with his own isolation: "I possessed no money, no friends, no kind of property. I was, besides, endued with a figure hideously deformed and loathsome. I was not even of the same nature as man. . . . Was I, then, a monster, a blot upon the earth, from which all men fled and whom all men disowned?" (116-117). The monster, then, stands in problematic relation with the social sphere, much as does his creator. Moreover, the doppelganger relation between Victor and the creature, as well as the unsolvable question as to which is the horrible monster (and which the romantic hero), are not unlike the economic ambivalences and ambiguities involving both the entrepreneur and his production, as they animate and disturb the marketplace.

The concept of the entrepreneur, then, establishes a baseline connection among various sites of "enterprise," including Walton's polar discoveries, Clerval's colonial trade, Victor's creative production, and even the monster's quest for recognition in the social sphere. While each of the major (male) characters—including the monster—is linked to an explicit economic content in *Frankenstein*, this content is repeatedly rendered as little more than a marginal consideration in their undertakings, just as it is serves as an instrumental body part in Shelley's gothic narrative. Yet we can explore this relation further by examining Shelley's representation of creativity, innovation, risk, profit and loss (or triumph and failure), mobility, secrecy, and detection. Moreover, all of these are affixed to bipolar valences of dread and desire that resemble a similar set of uncertainties *within* economic representations of the entrepreneur—a mixture of ambivalence and ambiguity that is, in turn, replicated in the transmogrified affiliations and exchanges *between* gothic and economic identities.

Walton, Clerval, and Victor are all variously represented as "divine wanderers" (28) who seek to "avoid the common pathways of men" (20). As with Walton's polar search and Clerval's colonialist ambitions, Victor's attempt to create life involves the desire to do something new. Yet like geographical exploration and colonialist enterprise, scientific discovery and technological innovation are not autonomous productions, nor are they attempts to create something out of nothing. In this sense, readings that focus on Victor's sexual ambivalence and his dream of creating life on his own tend to understate the extent to which Victor portrays himself (as does Shelley in describing her own authorial process) as one who recombines the factors of production in a manner that is far from autonomous or *ex nihilo*. He discusses at some length the role of his predecessors, his social resources and contexts, and the materials he utilizes and recombines. To repeat the observation made at the outset, Victor's story suggests something like a narrative about recycled garbage as much as it does a male procreation story. Specifically, Victor uses his own personal experiences (such as the lightning bolt), recovered dead body parts, and a motley of scientific discourses as factors of production that he recombines into an innovative formulation. When Victor tells Walton that to "examine the causes of life, we must first have recourse to death" (50), he underscores how his innovation makes collaborative use of that which has come and gone before it.

Throughout his description of his innovative production, Victor repeatedly underscores this recombinatory dialectic between the old and the new. Early in his youth he falls under the sway of the "chimerical" texts of ancient natural philosophers who, he tells Walton, were the "lords of my imagination" until an encounter with a lightning bolt and a discussion with a family guest about research in "electricity and galvanism" led him to "set down natural history and all its progeny as a deformed and abortive creation" (38-41). When he goes off to school, Professor Krempe reinforces this position by dismissing all his earlier studies as a waste of time. Victor cannot conceive of a connection between the old and the new discourses: "The ambition of the enquirer seemed to limit itself to the annihilation of those visions on which my interest in science was chiefly founded. I was required to exchange chimeras of boundless grandeur for realities of little worth" (46).

However, another Professor at Ingolstadt, M. Waldman, recombines the relation between the old and the new—chimera and reality—into a discourse that animates Victor. Attending M. Waldman's lecture, Victor is drawn to the professor's "aspect expressive of the greatest benevolence," and recalls his voice as "the sweetest I had ever heard" (46). Waldman announces that the moderns, "whose hands seem only made to dabble in dirt . . . have indeed performed miracles. They penetrate into the recesses of nature, and show how she works in her hiding-places. They ascend into the heavens . . . . They have acquired new and almost unlimited powers; they command . . . mimic . . . and even mock" the natural world (47). Waldman's "aspect" and discourse completely seduces Victor: "one by one the various keys were touched . . . chord after chord was sounded . . . . So much has been done . . . more, far more, will I achieve; treading in the steps already marked, I will pioneer a new way" (47). Victor does not return to his former enthusiasms, but they do animate his engagement in a new "modern" course of study, a combination that is made possible by Waldman's generous acknowledgement to Victor that the "labours of men of genius however erroneously directed, scarcely ever fail in ultimately turning to the solid advantage of mankind" (48).

This entrepreneurial recombination of old and new in the interest of progress is replicated in Victor's exploration of death and life, for it is in "examining and analyzing all the minutiae of causation, as exemplified in the change from life to death, and death to life" that Victor experiences "from the midst of this darkness a sudden light . . . so brilliant and wondrous, yet so simple, that . . . I was surprised, that among so many men of genius . . . I alone should be reserved to discover so astonishing a secret" (51). However, the "sudden light" notwithstanding, there is still much work to be done: "Not that, like a magic scene, it all opened upon me at once: the information I had obtained was of a nature rather to direct my endeavors" (51). At this point, he stands somewhere between the idea and the execution:

> When I found so astonishing a power placed within my hands, I hesitated a long time concerning the manner in which I should employ it. Although I possessed the capacity of bestowing animation, yet to prepare a frame for the reception of it . . . still remained a work of inconceivable difficulty and labour." (52)

While critics such as Montag have widely noted Shelley's lack of scientific and technical detail (one can only wonder what such a novel would look like), it is important to remember that Victor describes his workshop efforts not only in terms of romantic inspiration or biological birth, but also as a technological predicament: at the beginning he lacks the necessary materials, he encounters the "great hindrance" of "the minuteness of the parts" in the manufacturing process, he spends "some months collecting and arranging" materials, and he experiences a series of failures before ultimate success (52-3).

These technical challenges of invention are also rendered in terms of the trials of the economic workplace. His "cheek had grown pale" and his "person had become emaciated with confinement" as he experiences the "horrors of . . . secret toil." Moreover, in his description of the "workshop of filthy creation," he makes reference to "employment," "occupation," "work," and "unwholesome trade" (53-5). But in this version of the workplace, Victor's efforts do not resemble the determined activities and returns of the capitalist or the laborer. He not only possesses the factors of production and does the work, but also recombines and animates his materials into a new manufacturing enterprise, just as he assumes (or at least believes he does) the risks of innovative combination. Victor attempts to benefit society by pursuing an enterprise in which the desire for the "marvellous" (20, 29) commingles with a dreaded sense of the monstrous, a mix that creates the bipolar configurations of "prosperity or ruins" (41) that delineate the gothic economy. Put in strict economic terms, this novel imagines the returns on enterprise neither as the determined interest that accrues to capital, nor the certain wage payments to labor, nor the payment of rent on natural resources; instead, it suggests an uncertain profit-loss scenario of creative risk-taking. Entrepreneurial enterprise involves the coming together of all of the necessary factors—natural resources, labor, capital *and* the creative vision of the entrepreneur, who, like his production, flickers into existence upon the tableau of Shelley's narrative.

This relation between economic and gothic formations of dread and desire can be observed in Shelley's representation of mobility and open space in relation to secrecy and detection. Indeed, one of the key motifs in *Frankenstein* is pursuit, and Shelley manages to integrate a number of its aspects into a gothic landscape composed of various configurations of the supernatural, the sublime, and the pathological. Yet this depiction of pursuit also suggests a gothic fictional version of how economists describe the dialectic of the "creative destruction" of entrepreneurial production and its inevitable dissolution in the marketplace, for although the entrepreneur requires freedom and mobility to create his production of a difference, unless he can retain his production as a kind of protected secret, those same forces render this difference as that which is variously appropriated, integrated, and naturalized.

In this free-market entrepreneurial model, the freedom of agents and the mobility of resources are both productive and destructive. For while the freedom of the entrepreneur allows him to pursue an enterprise that would destroy the equilibrium of present conditions, this same freedom keeps the entrepreneur from enjoying control over his production. Unless he can maintain his innovative mode of production as a kind of secret, he cannot retain his ownership or protection of that entrepreneurial difference—patents expire, monopolies are challenged, and competition imitates innovation. Entrepreneurial profits are themselves both objects of desire for the individual entrepreneur and a kind of aberrant friction or pressure differential in the system that the market naturally tends to eliminate by means of various adjustment mechanisms. Formally speaking, the economic "chase" is about pursuing the "difference" or "abnormality" of profit and eliminating it. To restate the claim made earlier, the entrepreneur is a kind of free-ranging romantic hero in this market narrative, yet he also occupies an ironic or even tragic position of risk, isolation, and failure in a story whose resolution is always a return to zero.

This version of the entrepreneurial marketplace offers a way of reading the complicated plot structures and figurations involving Victor's enterprise, such as the switchback narrative patterns of pursuit and the contradictory valences associated with open and closed spaces. In the early stages of the story, Victor's pursuit involves his attempt to realize his innovative vision, for which he must be free to move about and to bring resources together in a new combination, yet he must also enclose himself off from others in order to maintain the secrecy of his production. Secrecy and detection are linked to Victor's desire for and dread of closed and open spaces, both of which are associated with his domestic and social relations, his workplace, and the natural landscapes. Victor is claustrophobic when bound by those domestic and social ties that would keep him from his enterprise. Yet his "enclosure" inside his secret space is precisely what maintains his entrepreneurial position. At the same time, his workshop undertaking paradoxically generates a similar sense of claustrophobia, with its associations of pursuing "nature to her hiding places" and the "horrors . . . of secret toil . . . among the unhallowed damps of the grave" (53). The isolation and alienation of the workshop are explicit:

> In a solitary chamber, or rather cell, at the top of the house, and separate from all the other apartments . . . I kept my workshop of filthy creation . . . . and often did my human nature turn with loathing from my occupation, whilst, still urged on by an eagerness which perpetually increased. (53)

Once the monster is produced, however, Victor faces a different predicament—the threat of open spaces and freedom of movement. So when Victor flees from this workshop enclosure, open spaces are also repeatedly reconfigured as sites of terror. It is as if the claustrophobia of the domestic household is somehow linked to the drive for enterprise, but Victor also experiences this claustrophobia in relation to his workshop, suggesting some compulsion for a freedom of movement that makes problematic any overdetermined literal distinction between the spheres of domesticity and work.[8] Moreover, although Victor seeks to escape from both sorts of claustrophobic entrapment, this desire for "open space" places him in sites of the romantic sublime that are transmogrified into scenes of gothic agoraphobia (a terror that repeatedly anticipates and then produces the monster).

While we can speculate from many points of view as to why Victor does not anticipate his response to the realization of his vision, and flees in horror once the creature's eye flickers open, an entrepreneurial heuristic offers two possible explanations. First, Victor recognizes that he has no way of maintaining control or ownership of the monster. The monster presents Victor with the problem of property, in which the monster is something like a manufacturing secret that Victor cannot patent or a text he cannot copyright, for Victor operates in a social and legal framework unable to recognize the monster as an economic identity, just as that framework can find no ontological place for the monster within the boundaries of its conventions and norms. In economic terms, Victor cannot make the successful transition from inventor to either capitalist (the owner of production) or entrepreneur. Interpretations of Victor as the Romantic artist might be both figuratively and historically linked to the economic predicament of the inventor-author-entrepreneur under the conditions of capitalist production.[9]

A second and somewhat diabolical explanation of Victor's response would be that he does not run away from the monster, so much as he seeks to assure its more extensive (and disruptive) introduction into the social sphere. That is, Victor's strategies of avoidance and secrecy insure the realization of monstrous destruction, as he leads the monster all over Europe and beyond. Victor's failures of oversight are, to deploy the pun, the stuff of successful entrepreneurial oversight, as the chase involves both the protection and circulation of his innovative production. Finally, as is discussed in the conclusion, this chase results in an ambiguous and ambivalent ending, for although it might be argued that Victor literally fails to introduce his production into the social sphere as an entrepreneurial success, he (or Shelley) somehow succeeds in placing it there, at least at the level of the social imagination. In this version, Walton might stand in as a narrative middle-man who helps to effect the circulation of Victor's undertaking, much as Shelley's gothic mediation conducts an economic content to her reader by way of her "hideous progeny."

Once Victor's undertaking actually produces the creature, "the beauty of the dream vanishe[s], and breathless horror and disgust" overwhelm him. After a night of "the wildest dreams" (56), he flees the workshop and seeks the free movement of the city streets: "I issued into the streets, pacing them with quick steps, as if I sought to avoid the wretch whom I feared every turning of the street would present to my view. I did not dare return to the apartment . . . but felt impelled to hurry on" (58). However, this public space gives him no comfort: "I traversed the streets without any clear conception of where I was going or what I was doing. My heart palpitated in the sickness of fear, and I hurried on with irregular steps" (58). Then the narrative uncannily produces the safety of a number of enclosures: "I came at length opposite an inn . . . . Here I paused, I knew not why; but remained some minutes with my eyes fixed on a coach that was coming toward me . . . . it stopped just where I was standing; and on the door being opened, I perceived Henry Clerval" (58). Clerval is, of course, a kind of emissary whose presence recalls for Frankenstein the enclosing safety of his domestic relations, which afford him a "calm and serene joy" (58). Ironically, Victor experiences the safety of a kind of domestic interiority just as Clerval has escaped his own: his father "has permitted [Clerval] to undertake a voyage of discovery to the land of knowledge" (59).

Victor's movements are temporarily suspended with the "commencement of a nervous fever" (60) that lasts for several months. His friend Clerval nurses him back to health, in part, it should be repeated, by means of a shared project of Orientalist studies, which Clerval sees as "affording scope for his spirit of enterprise" and in which Victor fulfills his need for "instruction [and] consolation" (67). Although he claims that he does "not contemplate making any other use of them than temporary amusement," he waxes rather oddly about their soothing melancholy, elevating joy, and the way in which in "their writings, life appears to consist in a warm sun and a garden of roses, in the smiles and frowns of a fair enemy, and the fire that consumes your own heart" (67), all of which feels like an unconscious reference to his own suppressed enterprise. Even this Orientalist expanse of sun and roses is linked to a claustrophobic dread.

In the spring, Clerval proposes a more "pedestrian tour in the environs of Ingolstadt," the first of a number of set pieces in which nature is romantically depicted. Clerval helps him to rediscover how this "aspect of nature" and social intercourse call forth the "better feelings of my heart," allowing him to see how a "selfish pursuit had cramped and narrowed me." Accordingly, nature presents a "serene sky and verdant fields" that fill him with "ecstasy." The season is "divine; the flowers of spring bloomed in the hedges." Even "the peasants were dancing, and everyone we met appeared gay and happy. My own spirits were high, and I bounded along with feelings of unbridled joy and hilarity" (68). Again, this is but one side of the bipolar equation of "prosperity or ruin" (41), both of which are associated with open and closed spaces. In this instance, open space and free movement are rendered in romantic pastoral terms that are completely outside the realm of his entrepreneurial "workshop of filthy creation." At the same time, we would not want to read this strictly as Shelley's romantic affirmation of the natural equilibrium in a pre-capitalist social order, for the open spaces of nature can turn ominous, as is evident in Victor's return home to Geneva upon hearing of the death of his brother: "I could hardly see the dark mountains .... The picture appeared a vast and dim scene of evil, and I foresaw dimly that I was destined to become the most wretched of human beings" (72). More precisely, this scene involves some sublime blend of terror and beauty:

> I saw the lightnings playing on the summit of Mont Blanc in the most beautiful of figures.... vivid flashes of lightning dazzled my eyes, illuminating the lake, making it appear like a vast sheet of fire; then for an instant every thing seemed of a pitchy darkness, until the eye recovered itself from the preceding flash.... I watched the tempest, so beautiful yet terrific. (73)

This account recalls the night of the creation of the monster, and in a gothic animation of the unconscious, the monster appears.

A similar romantic depiction of nature's terror and beauty is repeated after Justine's death when, "encompassed by a cloud which no beneficial influence could penetrate," Victor's "sullen despair" again drives him into the open spaces of the nearby Alpine valleys. As with his escape from his family to Ingolstadt and his walking tour with Clerval, Victor seeks "by change of place, some relief from [his] intolerable sensations" (91). Here Victor attempts to lose himself in the "magnificent and astonishing character" of the "singular beauty" of the "sublime" Alps. Yet as with his other escapes, whether Orientalist studies or earlier walking tours, these vistas stir Victor's unconscious preoccupation with the monster, as the mountains above appear to him as the "habitations of another race of beings" (91). This romantic detour goes on for two more days, with an increasing sense of the terrible as the weather turns bad and he attempts his ascent of the summit of Montanvert, which is "terrifically desolate." Eventually, the "severity of the scene" no longer affords a "tingling long-lost sense of pleasure," nor does it "subdu[e] and tranquillis[e]" his grief; instead, a "melancholy impression" overwhelms him (92-94). Then, in one more turn of the wheel, the vision of Mont Blanc produces a brief sense of euphoria: "My heart, which was before sorrowful, now swelled with something like joy; I exclaimed—'Wandering spirits, if indeed ye wander, and do not rest in your narrow beds, allow me this faint happiness, or take me, as your companion, away from the joys of life'" (95). At this moment the monster again appears, a "wandering spirit" indeed who moves at "superhuman speed" (95). The pattern of these two walking tours is repeated yet again when Victor and Clerval take a trip to Britain, as well as in the final chase at the pole. In each instance, desire for freedom of movement is transmogrified into a kind of agoraphobic landscape in which the scene is interrupted by the monster.

Another way of describing this aspect of the novel is to note how both the claustrophobia and agoraphobia are variously gendered. Victor's aversion to domestic relations, the nightmares involving his mother and Elizabeth during his laboratory work at Ingolstadt, and his disgust at creating a female companion for the monster all suggest an ambivalence toward gendered aspects of both biological reproduction and his own enterprise. The production of the female creature is especially problematic, for Victor's efforts to "compose a female" (145) transform him from an inspired creator of innovative production into an alienated laborer of a repetitive reproduction:

> I proceeded in my labour, [and] it became every day more horrible and irksome. Sometimes I could not prevail on myself to enter my laboratory for several days; and at other times I toiled day and night in order to complete my work. It was indeed a filthy process in which I was engaged. During my first experiment, a kind of enthusiastic frenzy had blinded me to the horror of my employment . . . . But now I went to it in cold blood, and my heart often sickened at the work of my hands. (158-159)

Victor's expansive enterprise now feels more like claustrophobic factory work. In the technical sense, this production involves nothing substantially innovative, suggesting the dissolution of the entrepreneurial function into a more determined labor, yet the female also signifies the risk of unforeseeable consequences, including the "creative destruction" of a new "race of devils" (160). Both the claustrophobia of this assembly line "reproduction of production" and the agoraphobia of the "open possibilities" that female labor might one day bring forth lead Victor to destroy her. The production and productivity of the female both resembles and undermines Victor's entrepreneurial agency and function. Unlike readings in which "masculinist" science, technology, and capitalist production are poised in opposition to the sphere of romantic nature, female domesticity and biological reproduction, the engendered economy of enterprise in *Frankenstein* points to a much more problematic formulation. Victor's unwillingness to create a female monster points not so much to a difference from his undertaking the production of a male monster, as to a repetition of a similar set of contradictions involving entrepreneurial innovation and control.

IV. ENTREPRENEURIAL PATENTS PENDING

Frankenstein begins with an authorial introduction that underscores Shelley's self-representation as an author-entrepreneur, although her readers have not been able to recognize this entrepreneurial formation in the body of her "hideous progeny" (10). It is as if the claustrophobia and agoraphobia that Victor experiences are replicated in the gothic transmogrification of this economic content, in which the novel and its readers together display a similar kind of agoraphobia—a word whose roots, we would do well to remember, refer to a fear of the marketplace.[10]

In her Introduction to the 1831 edition, Shelley begins with the question of the origin of the story. As does Victor in his account of his production, she asserts that the enterprise was neither autonomous nor instantaneous, and that it essentially involved a recombination of many resources—upbringing, exposure to previous works, a mix of social affiliation and personal isolation, creative inspiration and innovative elaboration and revision, and finally social presentation. In many ways, her account reads like a description of the entrepreneur in a market. First, she sets out to produce a story in response to a specific demand: "We will each write a ghost story," Lord Byron suggests in the summer of 1816 to the small group of friends that included the Shelleys (7). She even makes a distinction between her husband Percy's poetic sensibilities and the more prosaic ability "to invent the machinery of a story," thereby suggesting an implicit figurative connection between novelistic and industrial production. Shelley then attempts "to think of a story," yet experiences "that blank incapability of invention" (8). At this point, she offers an analysis of the nature of invention:

> Every thing must have a beginning . . . and that beginning must be linked to something that went before. . . . Invention, it must be humbly admitted, does not consist in creating out of void, but out of

> chaos; the materials must, in the first place, be afforded: it can give form to dark, shapeless substances, but cannot bring into being the substance itself. In all matters of discovery and invention, even of those that appertain to the imagination, we are continually reminded . . . [that i]nvention consists in the capacity of seizing on the capabilities of a subject: and in the power of molding and fashioning ideas suggested to it. (8)

Like the entrepreneur, the author-inventor must make use of and then recombine that "chaos" of all available factors of production into a novel configuration. This process is neither merely the labor of (re)production nor creation "out of void." Therefore, like Victor's story, which is full of references to pre-texts (e.g., Wordsworth, Coleridge, Goethe, Plutarch, Volney, and Milton), Shelley describes those influences that help produce the creative "inspiration" of her dream. After the dream, Shelley attempts "to exchange the ghastly image of my fancy for the realities around" (9), which also resembles Victor's entrepreneurial desire to transform creative invention into a socially viable innovation. Even in the "new and improved" 1831 edition, Shelley takes the opportunity to make one last entrepreneurial pitch: "And now, once again, I bid my hideous progeny go forth and prosper" (10).

This is not to suggest that any account of an individual's attempt (whether Shelley's or Victor's) to create something new necessarily suggests the freedom, risk, and innovation of the economic entrepreneur. Even if we were to narrow our scope to novelistic fiction, the representation of individualist effort and social progress are so pervasive as to raise the question of whether we ought to see in them a necessary relation to economic innovation in particular. However, I have sought to demonstrate that those more familiar subjects to which readers of *Frankenstein* have previously made reference, including literary creativity, scientific progress, social reform, crime, biological reproduction, and even economic production, can be profitably recombined into an entrepreneurial reading of *Frankenstein*. Moreover, I have proposed that the gothic transmogrification of this economic discourse is itself a kind of performance of entrepreneurial innovation. This relation between entrepreneurial and literary activity poses the problem of reading itself as we gather together the hermeneutic pieces, much as at the end of the story Victor's interpretation of his undertaking is structured and sustained by his inability to recognize his own identity as an entrepreneurial agent. He confesses to Walton:

> When I reflected on the work I had completed . . . I could not rank myself with the herd of common projectors. But this thought, which supported me in the commencement of my career, now serves only to plunge me lower in the dust. All my speculations and hopes are as nothing . . . . My imagination was vivid, my powers of analysis and application were intense; by the union of these qualities I conceived the idea, and executed the creation of a man. (204)

Victor's confession here reflects not only his deep-seated ambivalence, but also a faint background economic hum, with its vocabulary of "work," "projectors," "career," and "speculations." Yet this entrepreneurial current remains undetected by Victor, who cannot recognize the contradiction between the repudiation of his own work and his exhortation to the sailors who threaten mutiny against Walton and his enterprise:

> Are you so easily turned from your design? Did you not call this a glorious expedition . . . . because it was full of danger and terror . . . for this was an honourable undertaking. You were hereafter to be hailed as the benefactors of your species. . . . Oh! be men, or be more than men. Be steady to your purposes, and firm as a rock. This ice is not made of such stuff as your hearts may be; it is mutable, and cannot withstand you, if you say that it shall not. (207)

Even more problematic is Victor's final account and plea to Walton, which is so ambivalent and ambiguous as to be impossible to interpret conclusively. He again invokes an economic discourse when he tells Walton that his desire for the death of the monster is no longer tied to "that burning hatred" but is instead the result of a rational Benthamite analysis of social utility, in which he seeks to maximize the social good by weighing the happiness of the creature against that of society. He concludes that the claims of the latter are greater than those of the individual monster.[11] But this entire depiction of utility and responsibility is indecipherable:

> During these last days I have been occupied in examining my past conduct; nor do I find it blameable. In a fit of enthusiastic madness I created a rational creature, and was bound towards him, to assure, as far as was in my power, his happiness and well-being. This was my duty; but there was another still paramount to that. (209)

By "past conduct," does he refer to the act of "enthusiastic madness," to his initial sense of obligation to the creature, or to his eventual repudiation of the monster afterward? At what point is his measurement of social utility, for which he has made claims all along, verifiable? More problematically, does the "rational creature" who is produced by this madness refer only to the monster, or might it also suggest Victor himself, the utilitarian who continues to imagine that he can measure social benefit, but who really pursues his own self-interest projected outward and reified as the "invisible hand" of the monster? And if the repudiation of his own self-interest against the paramount claims of society beckons him to destroy the monster, what are we to make of his reminder to Walton that "actuated by selfish and vicious motives, I asked you to undertake my unfinished work" (209)? Does he refer to a selfish and vicious desire to create or to destroy the monster, both of which, he claims, have now been supplanted by a more rational utilitarian analysis?

Finally, when Victor tells Walton, "I renew this request now, when I am only induced by reason and virtue," is he telling him to destroy the monster or not? We ought not be too hasty in concluding the former, at least in some figurative or ideological sense, given these confusions and contradictions, which Victor himself acknowledges:

> my judgment and ideas are already disturbed by the near approach of death. I dare not ask you to do what I think right, for I may still be misled by passion. . . . Seek happiness in tranquillity, and avoid ambition, even if it be only the apparently innocent one of distinguishing yourself in science and discoveries. Yet why do I say this? I have myself been blasted in these hopes, yet another may succeed. (210)

Like the monster, the entrepreneur is never fully recognized or named in the fictional economy of Shelley's novel. Yet this naming is emblematic of the enterprise of reading itself, an undertaking among the fictional body parts that would recombine them into something new and useful.

NOTES

[1] See, for example, the collection of essays in George Levine and U. C. Knoepfmacher, eds., *The Endurance of Frankenstein: Essays on Mary Shelley's Novel*.

[2] The Oxford English Dictionary cites F. A. Walker's *Political Economy* (1883) as the first English appearance of the "entrepreneur" in political economy.

[3] For economic readings of *Frankenstein*, see, for example, Elsie Michie, "*Frankenstein* and Marx's Theories of Alienated Labor"; Franco Moretti, *Signs Taken for Wonders: Essays in the Sociology of Literary Forms;* and Warren Montag, " 'The Workshop of Filthy Creation': A Marxist Reading of *Frankenstein*." I discuss Michie's and Montag's readings of *Frankenstein* below.

[4] "Richard Cantillon and the Nationality of Political Economy," *Contemporary Review*, 1881. Qtd. in Schumpeter, 217.

[5] Although interest is more typically described as the reward of capital, references to profit underscore some of the confusion regarding capital and the returns to the "capitalist," which often denotes an implicit entrepreneurial element.

[6] See, for example, Schumpeter's *The Theory of Economic Development.*

[7] See Fredric Jameson, *The Political Unconscious: Narrative as a Socially Symbolic Act.*

[8] For two feminist readings of the domestic household, claustrophobia, and economic mobility, see Kate Ellis, "Monsters in the Garden: Mary Shelley and the Bourgeois Family," and Johanna M. Smith, " 'Cooped Up': Feminine Domesticity in *Frankenstein*."

[9] It would be interesting to pursue a reading of the monster in terms of patent and copyright law, both in terms of the monster as a literal instance of economic manufacture and as an allegorical figuration of the problem of authorial ownership of intellectual property. For example, the links between the Romantic version of the author and the evolution of copyright law are explored in Martha Woodmansee and Peter Jaszi, eds., *The Construction of Authorship: Textual Appropriation in Law and Literature* .

[10] From the Greek "agora" or marketplace. For a related analysis of the marketplace and open and closed spaces, see Gillian Brown's article on Herman Melville's *Bartleby the Scrivener* , "The Empire of Agoraphobia," in which she interprets Bartleby's desire for enclosure and the problematic relation between domestic and economic spheres.

[11] David Kaufmann provides an interesting reading of the novel and its relationship to classical political economy along these lines. In Kaufmann's view, classical economists sought to reconcile the claims of individual self-interest with social equity. He reads *Frankenstein* as a novelistic performance of these tensions. See especially Chapter 2, "Burke and Paine Meet *Frankenstein*: Novels and Economics between Revolution and Reform," *The Business of Common Life*, 30-64.

CHAPTER 4

The Difference of a Doubloon

The Oil of Trade in *Moby Dick*

> *"It is none of the wheels of trade: It is the oil which renders the motion of the wheels more smooth and easy."*
>
> -DAVID HUME, "OF MONEY" (309)

> *"Such a clearer! such a sweetener! such a softener! such a delicious mollifier!"*
>
> -*MOBY DICK* (322)

One morning not long after the Pequod has left Nantucket on its whaling expedition, Ahab paces back and forth upon the deck with an especially "nervous step" that leads Stubb to suspect that "the chick that's in him pecks the shell. 'Twill soon be out" (136). The hours wear on "with the same intense bigotry of purpose in his aspect," until near the close of day he comes to a halt on the deck, inserts his bone leg into the custom-fitted hole by the bulwarks, and orders Starbuck to assemble the crew. Reminding all hands of his earlier orders to keep an eye out for a white whale, Ahab holds up a "broad bright coin to the sun," a Spanish ounce of gold worth sixteen dollars, and promises this doubloon to "Whosoever of ye raises me a white-headed whale with a wrinkled brow and a crooked jaw . . . with three holes punctured in his starboard fluke" (138). Ahab makes quite a show of the doubloon in this announcement. After holding up it high to the sun, he rubs the gold piece "against the skirt of his jacket, as if to heighten its lustre, and without any words was meanwhile lowly humming to himself, producing a sound so strangely muffled and inarticulate that it seemed the mechanical humming of the wheels of his vitality in him" (137-8). Then he takes a maul from Starbuck and dramatically nails the doubloon to the main-mast as he states the terms of its possession. The entire crew can now gaze at it with longing (and perhaps a little dread as well), keeping one eye on it, as it were, while keeping the other peeled for signs of the whale, for they immediately understand that their whaling venture has become a quest for Moby Dick, the legendary leviathan that "razeed" Ahab and made him a "poor pegging lubber."

We, too, ought to keep our eye on the doubloon, for it is with Ahab's introduction of the doubloon into the Pequod's economy that he first announces his intention and then seeks to insure its realization. Ahab's infusion of money into this system is ostensibly an attempt to produce the talismanic white whale instead of the more pedestrian blubbery goods sought by the "Nantucket market," for which he does not give a "Hoot!" (139). With the doubloon, then, Ahab attempts to make a real difference in the direction of the ship's enterprise. A question to ask, therefore, is whether this doubloon indeed makes a difference, and what the nature of this difference might be. Moreover, since the doubloon is a monetary figure, we can approach this problem as an economic one, by considering how, in the history of economic analysis, economists have posed a similar set of questions: What is the role of money, and what real difference does money make?

When Starbuck objects that Ahab's venture "will not fetch thee much in our Nantucket market," Ahab replies, "come closer, Starbuck; thou requirest a little lower layer. If money's to be the measurer, man, and the accountants have computed their great countinghouse the globe, by girdling it with guineas . . . then, let me tell thee, that my vengeance will fetch a great premium *here*," striking himself in the chest (139). Ahab's position is somewhat contradictory, since he uses money to effect a transaction and direct the Pequod toward a desired outcome, yet he dismisses money as a kind of nominal banality. Like Starbuck, then, we need to go to a "little lower layer" to appreciate the relation between a world girdled with guineas and the doublooned economy of *Moby Dick*.

From a number of perspectives, we could say that the doubloon makes no material difference. First, while the doubloon conveniently allows Ahab to name his purpose, it does not cause or alter those intentions. The chase is, as it were, a done deal, for Ahab has already made up his mind and will allow neither the fears of his crew nor the interests of the owners to deter him: "What cares Ahab? Owners, owners? Thou art always prating to me, Starbuck, about those miserly owners, as if the owners were my conscience. But look ye, the only real owner of anything is its commander" (363). Second, to reiterate the point made above, Ahab himself privately dismisses the importance of money to Starbuck, as he insists that the white whale is a kind of metaphysical mint possessing a much greater value. At best, the doubloon would seem to be a convenient monetary trick he plays on the crew to rally it to undertake his quest. Third, although the doubloon ostensibly determines a change in purpose in most of the crew (with their cry of "Huzza! huzza!" upon Ahab's posting of the gold and his plans), the real bargain seems struck in the series of rituals Ahab proceeds to consummate with them—passing the pewter flagon of spirits for all to drink, grasping the crossed lances of his mates (to whom he conveys the charge of his "own electric thing"), and instructing the mates to fill the sockets of the harpooneers' killing "irons," who then drink as if from chalices. Indeed, the doubloon would seem to pale in comparison with the drink that is "as hot as Satan's hoof" and the pagan-like ritual acts by which Ahab passes his vision into the others in order to whip the crew into a killing frenzy. Finally, since he is ultimately the one who sights Moby Dick anyway, Ahab himself affirms that the difference of the doubloon is all for nought insofar as it can belong to no other: although Tashtego will insist that he saw the whale "almost the same instant," Ahab replies, "Not the same instant; not the same—no, the doubloon is mine, Fate reserved the doubloon for me. I only; none of ye could have raised the White Whale first" (411). In all these senses, the doubloon plays a seemingly neutral or merely nominal role in this enterprise.

And yet this doubloon figures importantly in Melville's fiction, for it serves as a monetary cynosure by which are configured a store of motifs that circulate throughout the novel, such as navels, eyes, suns, compasses, origins, the decipherability of texts, the signification and subjectivity of value, the material substances of representation, Orientalism, solipsism, international exchange, and universal transcendence (all this and more for just sixteen dollars!). These motifs are themselves all posted in Chapter 99, "The Doubloon" (331-6). For example, Ahab's "riveted glance" is "fastened upon the riveted gold coin" with the "same aspect of nailed firmness" that also characterizes his staring gaze "pointed [on] the needle in the compass" which charts his course. For Ahab is "newly attracted by the strange figures and inscriptions stamped on [the doubloon], as though now for the first time beginning to interpret for himself in some monomaniac way whatever significance might lurk in them." These inscriptions, in turn, are rendered as a series of Orientalist figurations, yet in his attempts to decipher them, Ahab sees only himself reflected there ("all are Ahab").[1] Several members of the crew also take turns interpreting the doubloon, whose value, while grounded in gold, is nevertheless afloat in a fiat of subjective signification ("There's another rendering now; but still one text," Stubb thinks). Finally, the mad cabin-boy Pip declares that the doubloon is the "ship's navel," underscoring its centrality as an object of both dread and desire.

The doubloon indeed suggests a kind of signifying paydirt toward which an interpretation of *Moby Dick* might be drawn, for this inscribed coin stands in for much of what the novel seems to be about, with its emphasis on the materials and metaphysics of meaning-making. Furthermore, since the doubloon is a monetary image, it points to a series of analogies between economic and fictional representation more broadly. For example, what are the similarities between money and fiction as representational systems? Upon what systems of value are they grounded? Do they passively reflect or actively shape reality? What role do their representational materials (e.g., metal, paper, writing) play in their capacities as signifying systems? And what is the relation between monetary representation and a fiction that self-reflexively brings such monetary tropes to our attention?

Readers of nineteenth-century American fiction have explored these and other questions about money in relation to language and literature, and have widely deployed monetary concepts in their analyses of fictional form and content. For example, in *Money, Language, and Thought*, Marc Shell examines a range of connections between monetary and linguistic representation in western thought and literature, such as in his analysis of nineteenth-century debates about metal and paper currency. Similarly, in *Money and Fiction: Literary Realism in the Nineteenth and Early Twentieth Centuries*, John Vernon argues for a variety of links between literary realism and monetary representation, such as the ability of paper to represent reality, money as an agent of social change and narrative development, and monetary debt as a trope for the production of novelistic temporality. In *The Gold Standard and the Logic of Naturalism*, Walter Benn Michaels explores connections between naturalist fiction and the gold standard, in which the paradoxical status of gold as both a "real" commodity and a monetary signifier is similarly performed in the naturalist attempt to represent the real by means of writing, a built-in contradiction that poses a kind of supplementarity or "internal difference" upon which naturalism is structured and sustained.[2]

These monetary readings of American literature are instances of a broader critical tradition examining links between money and language, which is predictable and productive, given how these subjects raise similar questions about value and representation. Moreover, novelistic fiction, with its registrations of capitalist conditions, is an especially likely place to encounter money as an important concern. Lionel Trilling, for example, proposes in *The Liberal Imagination* that "the novel is born with the appearance of money as a social element" (203). Edward W. Said similarly claims that "[m]oney is always in evidence during the course of the realistic novel" (*Beginnings*, 145). And as is reflected in the examples of Shell, Vernon, and Michaels, the critical purchase on money in fiction can be had not only in terms of literal subject matter, but also as a sometimes self-reflexive or more deeply embedded aspect of fictional representation. Again, these more intricate links tend to direct our attention to how some relation between fiction and the world resembles a similar connection between money and the economy, especially in terms of analogous sets of questions involving the stuff of signification and its relation to the real. Each of these critics, for example, has underscored the importance of nineteenth-century discourse about metal vs. paper monetary standards, and seen in this discourse a similar problematic involving the representational capacities of literary fiction. Yet we ought not to focus only on this particular aspect of money in our readings of fiction, and thereby limit our monetary interpretations to versions of the long-standing conversation about metal standards and paper fiat (which go back well beyond the nineteenth century). For while as committed readers of paper we might indeed be drawn to such controversies, economists arguably have been even more interested in a different debate that provides another useful way of approaching the relation between Melville's monetary and novelistic representations.

In formal economic analysis, a question that is related to, but different from, the problem of monetary standards has concerned economists at least as far back as the mercantilists of the seventeenth century and as recently as the contemporary monetarist school of "rational expectations": what effect does money—whatever the material form it might take or the inscriptions written upon it—have on "real" economic conditions, such as employment, output, distribution, and consumption? What real difference, as it were, does money make beyond its own representational function to nominally render real economic values? Throughout the history of economic thought, we encounter various formulations and related aspects of this question, in which money is said both to have a real effect on those conditions and, conversely, to function as an essentially neutral or merely nominal signifier of real economic outcomes. Most economists would agree that money makes at least some real difference, if by no other means than its basic functions as a measure of value, a store of value, and a medium of exchange. These are the functions by which money (as David Hume put it) oils the wheels of trade. If money does nothing else than facilitate transactions, for example, it has a real impact on economic outcomes.

The quantity theory of money proposes a fundamental relation between money supply and prices: changes in money supply result in a corresponding change in price levels. All things being equal, more doubloons, as it were, means higher prices for whales. However, the question this equation raises is, So what? Does a change in the money supply affect only prices? Do changes in money supply and prices involve merely a neutral indexing of a set of economic conditions, or do they actually determine the realization of those conditions? Again, does money make a real difference or a nominal one?

This line of economic inquiry resembles a question we can ask about what could be called the romantic nominalization of the whaling economy in *Moby Dick*. For the novel does not merely *represent* these economic conditions by way of a romantic currency, insofar as certain aspects of this metaphysical romance oil the wheels of trade to *realize* a version of an international free-trade economy. The literal and local subject matter of whaling is nominally represented in such a way that the economic realm is rendered in a discursive solvent of universal values and transcendent meanings, thereby establishing a "coincidence of wants" between romance and international exchange. The world girdled with guineas that Ahab scorns is not entirely disconnected from the doubiooned economy in which he would participate. Similarly, Ishmael (like Ahab and Melville) can dip his hands into the "delicious mollifier" of the stuff of whales and render it as a universal and transcendent liquidity (like a kind of money) because whaling is itself "always already" rendered in such a way as to imagine that such real dipping and handholding and squeezing is indeed possible.

Just as Ahab attempts to oil the wheels of his machinations with the doubloon, so too does Melville imagine the realization of an international economy whose real business would seem to be not the job of gathering whale oil so much as rendering it into the stuff of allegorical meaning-making. This universalizing discourse, however, has affinities and affiliations with the realization of the world economy as a unified system by which international identities and relations can be freely exchanged. When David Hume staked out an early position in monetary theory by claiming that money is not a wheel of trade but the oil that turns the wheels more effectively, he hedged his bet somewhat, for the oil still makes a real difference. Similarly, whaling twice-rendered—first from the real work of lubbering for blubber to the manufactured stuff of fiction and then to an even more universal and transcendent Melvillian solvency—serves up a kind of monetized fictional economy whose own mollifying wheels are not entirely set apart from those of the real one from which they would turn.

II. ECONOMIC EXTRACTS (RENDERED BY A SUB-SUB-ECONOMIST)

In order to offer a "valuable . . . bird's eye view of what has been promiscuously said, thought, fancied, and sung of the Leviathan," Melville opens with an assortment of "higgledy-piggledy whale statements" ostensibly collected by a "burrower and grubworm of a poor devil of a Sub-Sub" librarian (11). And although Melville laments the aspirations of all would-be members of "that hopeless, sallow tribe" of researchers ("Give it up, Sub-Subs!"), a short overview of some pertinent extracts of economic analysis provides a helpful framework for a monetary reading of the fictional economy of *Moby Dick.* Also, it should be noted that the references to *Moby Dick* in this "sub-sub" survey of monetary theory are not yet intended to produce a single sustained reading of the novel, for I take Ishmael's hermeneutic restlessness as my model and shift happily through a series of interpretive possibilities; in other words, the Melvillian anecdotes and analogies are deployed in this section chiefly to illustrate the economic analysis, as well as to begin to suggest how those figurations of money and trade surface in the novel.

When Ahab introduces an Ecuadorian doubloon into the economy of the Pequod, he performs an act that recalls an economic event referred to in early monetary theory, for the infusion of colonial Spanish precious metals taken from the Americas and put into circulation in Europe plays a notable role in early pre-classical analyses of the role of the money supply in the economy. In the sixteenth century England experienced a general increase in the level of prices, an inflationary climb that has come to be widely referred to as the "price revolution" and whose causes and effects have been debated ever since.[3] In the pre-classical and classical periods, political economists widely referred to this infusion of precious metals as a vivid and concrete historical example of how an increase in the money supply would push up prices.[4] Such a view would suggest that Ahab's introduction of the doubloon raises at least the nominal value of the whale in whatever economy in which both the money and the commodity might circulate.

However, the real importance of a change in the quantity of money was itself a key area of debate in early modern political economy. This debate can be framed in part as the difference between mercantilist and free-trade positions regarding the relationship between money and national wealth. Put broadly, mercantilist political economists of the seventeenth and eighteenth centuries believed that the source of national wealth was critically tied to the stockpiling of bullion, as if the national economy were a kind of whale ship that ought to hoard as much of the "oil of trade" as possible. This store of gold would be maximized if a nation maintained a positive trade balance, in which exported goods exceeded imports, hence the desirability of protectionist trade policies. For example, if imports were restricted to raw materials as much as possible, and if only surplus finished goods were exported, then (since finished goods tend to have a higher value than raw materials) these protectionist policies would create trade surpluses and a net inflow of gold.[5]

In whaling terms, the mercantile national ship scours international waters in search of whales, renders the whales into oil, then trades this oil for gold. Yet in *Moby Dick* the stuff of the whale is not just a commodity that is variously hoarded or traded, for it also functions much like gold itself insofar as the whale operates as a sort of general equivalent or central signifier by which an entire fictional economy of values are nominalized. Much as Pip describes the gold doubloon as the navel of the ship, so too does Ishmael insist that whaling is the "mother" (100) by which is produced and represented the offspring of his entire narrative. Melville's depiction of the gold doubloon, as a "real" commodity with a "killing wonderful" capacity to represent a whole system of values, resembles the monetization of whaling in *Moby Dick*, by which the whale attains a status as signifying specie in Melville's fictional economy. Although Ahab dismisses the value of the gold, a kind of quasi-mercantilist position nevertheless surfaces in the novel's monetized representation of whale oil as both a commodity and a standard of value. Still again, the objection that Ahab would willingly forego *this* oil of trade for the greater premium of Moby Dick overlooks the analogous configuration whereby the white whale—as the particular identity that can represent a whole system of values—is also monetized insofar is it represents an even greater signifying capability. In sum, the mercantilist formation in *Moby Dick* can be seen not only in its literal figuration of gold, but also in its respective figurative monetizations of whaling and the whale. The Pequod is, as it were, a mercantilist whaler searching for white gold.

In the mercantilist view, gold makes a real difference, for the greater the quantity of money held in the form of gold stockpiles, the greater the national wealth. While this "non-neutral" view of gold, real wealth, and protectionist trade policies generally held sway in the mercantile period, a number of political economists at that time (such as John Locke, Richard Cantillon, and David Hume) observed a problem with this desire for a sustained trade surplus and gold inflow over a long and indefinite period. They argued as follows: If a nation runs a trade surplus, the domestic money supply (gold) would increase. With this increase in the money supply come higher domestic prices (in contemporary parlance, more dollars chasing fewer goods). As a nation's commodity prices become higher relative to other nations' prices, foreign demand for that nation's exports drops, which would lead to a decline in both the outflow of goods and the inflow of gold. At the same time, relatively lower foreign prices would tend to increase a nation's commodity imports and gold exports. This process would generate a net outflow of gold and a trade deficit, which would again lower domestic prices and reverse the cycle. In this sense, attempting to create real wealth by hoarding gold is foiled by international market pricing mechanisms that render changes in the money supply neutral with respect to real economic outcomes.

This aspect of international trade and prices explains in part why money supply and prices move in tandem (whether in a self-contained economy or in a scenario of international exchange). The quantity theory of money (again, the relation between money supply and prices) therefore has ramifications for international trade, which the mercantilists were slow to see. For if the money supply only affects prices, which are merely nominal indexes of real conditions, it makes little sense to attempt to increase national wealth by increasing the supply of gold. The "neutral" theory of the quantity of money tends to challenge the mercantilist position that money makes a real difference in the creation of real wealth. In terms of the whaling world of *Moby Dick*, the fetishized desire for the gold doubloon *and* the white whale, which are both commodified and monetized, distracts the errant mercantilist ship from focusing on the real commodity production of whale oil (Starbuck's Nantucket market), hence its inability to realize economic wealth. Gold is, in this view, a sort of watery white elephant.

Classical economists challenged this mercantilist emphasis on gold, turning away from the nominal role of money and focusing instead on what they considered the sources of the "real" creation of wealth, hence Adam Smith's classical critique of mercantilist protectionism and his argument for free trade: real wealth comes from all nations producing what will bring the greatest relative returns, and exchanging their outputs with each other toward the benefit of all. Instead of protecting domestic industries, artificially maintaining a positive balance of trade, and hoarding gold, a nation should produce only what it can do better than others, or at least direct its factors of production where its opportunity costs are minimized. In this sense, we could read Ahab not as a mercantilist, but as an inspired entrepreneurial free-trader. As Ahab puts it to Starbuck (echoing Ricardo's notion of comparative advantage[6]), why not leave the less profitable whaling to others when you have bigger and better fish to fry? That is to say, the opportunity cost of whaling is, for Ahab, the white whale itself, a much too high a price for wasting time and resources participating in the "Nantucket market," for which Ahab does not give a "Hoot!" (139). In this interpretation, Ahab's quest suggests neither a mercantilist mistake nor the effacement of an economic configuration altogether, but instead a kind of free-trade quest in which the highest "premium" is to be possessed by leaving off the protected sea lanes of trade and pursuing greater returns elsewhere. Starbuck's challenge to Ahab need not be read as a literal objection to abandoning the economic enterprise of whaling, so much as the "intolerable . . . doltish stare" (139) of the mercantilist who cannot apprehend Ahab's rejection of his flawed notion about gathering wealth. Moby Dick is in this view neither commodified money nor a monetized commodity, but a new kind of real wealth to be pursued in opposition to the constraints or protections of mercantilist conventions.[7]

It would be inaccurate to depict the debate about the neutrality of money as the difference between mercantilism and classical political economy. As already noted, economists of all stripes acknowledge that a certain amount of money is necessary for transactional purposes, so it indeed is not entirely "neutral" in its relation to real economic outcomes. Even Hume, it should be remembered, who provided an early articulation of the challenge to mercantilist arguments for hoarding gold, acknowledged that money oils the wheels of exchange, hence it indeed makes a real difference in trade. Moreover, from Cantillon to Keynes to the current day, economists have explored how money can have an impact on real economic consequences (such as output and employment) in various short- and long-term scenarios. The pre-classical economist Richard Cantillon, for example, noted the distinction between relative prices within, and overall price levels of, an economy, pointing out that how the money supply enters into the economy—who has it and how they spend it (e.g., consumer spenders vs. capital investors)—would have a real effect on economic outcomes. Similarly, classical economists such as Henry Thornton and John Stuart Mill explored a variety of "non-neutral" aspects of changes in the money supply.[8] In terms of the doubloon, we would therefore ask not only whether its presence makes a difference, but also how that difference is determined and delineated by its mode of introduction into the Pequod's economy. Had Ahab introduced it as the reward for whale oil for the Nantucket market, it would have been a much different whaling story.

Since the classical period, of course, much attention has been given to money. John Maynard Keynes, for example, defended much of the mercantilist position about money and growth, and argued for a connection between their insights and his own analysis of the relationship between money supply, interest rates, demand, and employment. And neoclassical analysis both before and after Keynes has variously examined the real mechanisms that link money supply and price level. For example, Irving Fisher elaborated on the role of the velocity of money, in which both the money stock and the rate at which it changes hands or "turns over" play a role in price levels. In terms of *Moby Dick*, the price of the whale would be a function of both the quantity of doubloons and the velocity in which they move through the Pequod economy. While Ahab's single doubloon represents a given monetary stock that is literally posted in place, it nevertheless has a kind of velocity as it "changes hands" by passing from the consciousness of one individual to another, a monetary circulation that results in a kind of metaphysical inflation whereby more meanings chase a limited stock of real referents. As various members of the crew contemplate the meaning of the doubloon, it has the effect of several doubloons circulating and driving up the nominal prices (or proliferating the meanings) of that which it would variously represent.

More recently, the monetarist theory of "rational expectations" has attempted to show how the decisions of all economic participants are formulated in part by informed expectations about the future. As a result, attempts to affect the economy by adjusting the money supply are hampered because people already have anticipated those adjustments and acted accordingly. In terms of *Moby Dick*, the argument would be that Ahab's attempt to trick the crew and change their course by introducing the doubloon is ineffective, because they have somehow factored in this monetary bribe and have made adjustments for the possibility of going after the whale anyway (remember, Ahab admits that they've already heard mention of the white whale, just as the reader earlier encounters a number of foreshadowing clues). In this interpretation, all of Ahab's attempts to steer the Pequod along a desired course with the doubloon amount to a kind of unsuccessful or redundant monetary intervention, as if all the Ahabian tricks involving quadrants and needles were but the tools of a Keynesian monomaniac that could at best only resolve one crash with another.

To repeat the point made at the outset of this section, my admittedly anecdotal and allegorical monetizing of *Moby Dick* serves up a rather Ishmaelian motley of monetary meanings that can only arrive at the same sort of split vision that he observes in the whale and which he takes as his discursive model (261). Yet if we go along with Ahab's call to go to a "little lower layer," we can see how the representation of money in *Moby Dick* does not depict a single economic position (e.g., mercantilist vs. free-trade discourse, or neutralist vs. non-neutralist monetary theory); instead, a range of monetary figurations reflect and participate in the metaphysical and romantic nominalization of Melville's fictional economy as a site of universal and transcendent values and meanings.

If we read the doubloon as a monetary trope for Melville's romantic nominalizations of whaling more broadly, the question of monetary neutrality can be revised in terms of the relation between romantic representation and economic reality. Much as the stuff of whales is itself rendered into oil in the try-works of the Pequod, Melville invites us to "strike through the pasteboard mask" of economic enterprise in order to grab hold and squeeze out the nominal meanings that lie beyond it. Yet the monetization of the doubloon and the whale produce a romantic nominalization of international economy that makes the realization of this economic subject matter possible in the first place. In order to pursue this relation between monetary and romantic representation further, we can look to a variety of (Orientalized) colonial identities that are monetized and romantically inscribed. Like the doubloon and the whale, the colonial subject serves as a signifier of value that oils the wheels of international free trade.

Mercantilist protectionists and classical free-trade proponents alike looked to colonial exchange as an important area by which they could put forth their claims about the realization of national wealth in the context of international trade. In *Moby Dick* we encounter a similar configuration whereby colonial discourse is crucial in rendering the economy of the Pequod as a kind of domestic *and* universal household located within—and made possible by—a system of international exchange. This can be seen in how Melville renders the doubloon as a monetary text whose inscriptions suggest a number of Orientalist figurations that similarly circulate in relation to the colonial subjects on board the ship (especially Queequeg).

III. MERCANTILIST AND FREE-TRADE COLONIALISM

In Adam Smith's classical model of a self-regulating market, sellers and buyers of economic resources and commodities are free to engage in production, exchange, and consumption according to their own interests, and in this way the "invisible hand" of market forces arrives at economic efficiency and equity. Owners of the factors of production (land, labor, capital), for example, direct their resources to the highest bidder, and the returns they receive (rent, wages, profits) reflect the value they provide, much as the "financial lays" of the Pequod are assigned according to the contributions of the participants of the enterprise. Market prices, outputs, and distribution are all signifiers in a mechanistic system that arrives at a "natural" equilibrium in which both individual and social benefits are maximized. In this classical model, any attempt to regulate or constrain economic activity by way of protective tariffs or artificial monopolies results in inefficiency and inequity. This is essentially Smith's free-trade complaint against mercantilism.

In *Wealth of Nations*, the bulk of this critique of mercantilism occurs in Book IV. Smith attempts to demonstrate that mercantilist restraints of trade fail to serve the national interest. While much of this has to do with theories about the connections among trade balance, money, and wealth, Smith's argument takes an interesting turn in Chapter VII, in which he addresses at great length (some 85 pages) the question of those most protected and monopolized of trading partners, the colonies. Essentially, Smith argues that the most successful colonies are those that have been allowed the most freedom to trade whatever and with whomever they desire. Moreover, according to Smith, restrictions on the colonies that are intended to benefit the mother country actually hurt those domestic interests. Again, Smith's model suggests an economic hydraulics in which any tampering with the "natural" market mechanisms of price, output, and distribution necessarily creates inefficiencies and inequities. In terms of the Pequod, the colonial harpooneers should be paid their full market value in order to maximize the returns of this domestic interest.

In his analysis, Smith begins with the claim that colonial monopolies stunt growth, and as an example he argues that England's relative success compared with other European nations in the American colonies is linked to its more "open" trade policy (576-7), although he grants that such trade policies still involved protectionist elements (especially with regard to domestic manufactured goods). Citing the example of England's control over American tobacco exports, Smith argues that while such a monopoly may give the appearance of a relative advantage over other countries, it depresses the absolute advantage that would accrue to all nations by way of more efficient distribution (594-5). Central to such a model is the notion that monopolies of this sort create artificial profits, which then distort international capital flow by attracting capitalists toward these "deranged" profitable returns. These mercantilist "derangements," in turn, create inefficiencies throughout the marketplace. Giving Ishmael a harpoon to prop up domestic employment would be bad business indeed.

Smith makes a distinction between "the effects of the colony trade and those of the monopoly of that trade," for the "former are always and necessarily beneficial; the latter always and necessarily hurtful" (607). Moreover, because the benefits of colonial trade outweigh the monopolies' hurtful effects, Smith argues that there is a tendency to conflate the two and to assume that the latter are beneficial too. Smith proposes that the advantages of colonialism would be greatly enhanced for everybody if a free-trade policy were pursued. Notice that in this distinction, Smith does not address the political formations of colonialism itself; instead, he envisions the international economy as a single unified system of trading partners in which colonies are not so much "inside" the domestic imperial system as they are inside a much larger international system of free-market exchange. For the classical economists, the arguments for free trade operate at all levels of economic activity, involving a kind of romance of free exchange among individuals, groups within a nation's borders (between, for example, town and country), sovereign nations, and sovereign nations and colonies. Although the owners of the Pequod seek to exploit domestic and foreign workers alike (e.g., Ishmael's "three-hundredth lay"), and are especially loath even to hire an unconverted cannibal with no "papers," once they see Queequeg's real market worth, they hurry to pay him full market value.

As he does throughout *Wealth of Nations*, Smith acknowledges that individuals will often attempt to conspire against the national interest for personal gain. Colonial monopolies are one such instance: "It is thus that the single advantage which the monopoly procures to a single order of men is in many different ways hurtful to the general interest of the country" (613). Smith then goes on to satirize mercantilistic claims for colonialist protectionism:

> To found a great empire for the sole purpose of raising up a people of customers, may at first sight appear a project fit only for a nation of shopkeepers. It is, however, a project altogether unfit for a nation of shopkeepers; but extremely fit for a nation whose government is influenced by a shopkeepers. (613)

The term Smith employs for these skewed colonial relations is "derangement," which suggests not only a normative description of monopolist exploitation, but also a more formal positive account of the mechanistic distortions that these protections create in capital flows, resource distribution, profit returns, and growth:

> All the different regulations of a mercantile system, necessarily derange more or less this natural and most advantageous distribution of stock. But those which concern the trade to America and the East Indies derange it perhaps more than any other; because the trade to those two great continents absorbs a greater quantity of stock than any two other branches of trade. . . . Monopoly of one kind or another, indeed, seems to be the sole engine of the mercantile system. (630)

Smith, then, re-imagines colonial exchange not as a model for monopolistic and exploitative trade, which is self-defeating, but as the open and free exchange that allows the "natural" mechanisms of the market to realize the full possibilities of international economy.

While mercantilist sensibilities are variously manifest in *Moby Dick*, ultimately colonial identities, differences, and exchange figure heavily in the representation and realization of a free-trade version of international economy. For example, while Chapter 101 ("The Decanter") perhaps could just as well have been called "A Storehouse of Mercantilist Spirits," it nevertheless establishes a connection between international economy and Ishmael's universalizing metaphysics. This chapter follows the encounter with the English ship Samuel Enderby, which, like the meeting with the French whaler Rose-bud (*Bouton de Rose*) in Chapter 91, is something of a parody of trade relations in which American interests and cunning are in competition with European counterparts. The Enderby recalls for Ishmael the "original of the famous whaling house of Enderby & Sons," which, according to Ishmael, in 1775 "fitted out the first English ships that ever regularly hunted the Sperm Whale" (341), a date that allows Ishmael to assert a strong American presence in the whaling industry for at least fifty years before the English. However, in

1778 the English ship Amelia "was the first among the nations" to go around Cape Horn into the "great South sea," after which it returned to her domestic "berth with her hold full of the precious sperm . . . [and] was soon followed by other ships, English and American, and thus the vast Sperm Whale grounds of the Pacific were thrown open." Nor is this quite a description of competitive free-trade, for Ishmael explains that under the "immediate auspices" of the "indefatigable house . . . of Samuel and all his Sons, and partly, I think, at their expense, the British government was induced to send the sloop-of-war Rattler on a whaling voyage of discovery into the South Sea" (341-2). Moreover, in 1819 the same house "fitted out a discovery whale ship of their own, to go on a tasting cruise to the remote waters of Japan" (342), thereby suggesting how the development of mercantilist monopolies is tied to military presence and imperialist expansion: sometimes the invisible hand wears a protective glove.

Ishmael recounts a night of drinking and eating aboard the Enderby "long, very long after old Ahab touched her planks with his ivory heel" (342), and this allows him to note the exceptional "incidental and particular" hospitality of English whalers who, unlike their merchant kinsmen, have carried on with the "fat old fashions" of the "Hollanders, Zealanders, and Danes" who preceded them into the "whale fishery" (343). Ishmael's account of his "researches in the Leviathonic histories" presents a number of playfully complicated economic configurations. He tells of stumbling upon "an ancient Dutch volume" whose title is "Dan Coopman," which Ishmael takes as the name of a whaling cooper (the one who makes and repairs wooden casks). However, Ishmael's friend Dr. Snodhead, who translates the work for Ishmael in exchange for a box of sperm candles (whale as wax money), tells Ishmael that "Dan Coopman" means "The Merchant": "In short, this . . . book treated of the commerce of Holland; and among other subjects, contained a very interesting account of its whale fishery" (343).

This movement from the whaling ship's stash to the wide world of commerce only returns Ishmael into the "larders and cellars" of the ship, for one chapter in "Dan Coopman" captures his eye, a formidably extensive inventory of food and drink carried by the Dutch whalers. While admitting that "[m]ost statistical tables are parchingly dry in the reading," Ishmael's survey of the booty in the ship resembles the mercantilist innovation of national economic accounting.[9] That is to say, like the mercantilists who increasingly articulated the concept of national wealth as an object of study, Ishmael attempts to discover some meaning in—and then beyond—the numbers: "I devoted three days to the studious digesting of this beer, beef, and bread, during which many profound thoughts were incidentally suggested to me, capable of a transcendental and Platonic application; and, furthermore, I compiled supplementary tables of my own, touching the probable quantity of stock-fish, [etc.]" (344). In this way, Ishmael attempts to interpret the links among national wealth, international economy, and "transcendental and Platonic" values to be found in the economic ciphering of whaling.

In "The Decanter" (as in *Moby Dick* more generally), whaling is both instance of and symbol for the international economy. Moreover, those real conditions also have meaning or value beyond the literally economic, carrying Ishmael into abstraction and universalizing speculations. Ishmael's metaphysical nominalization of butter and beef and booze resembles the economic analysis of national wealth, as well as those collateral concepts and policies that would represent all the national economies of the world in terms of a unified and interdependent system of production, exchange, and consumption of value. Melville's monetization of the real, as rendered in his representation of whaling as the universal index, does not merely facilitate the representation of trade, but is itself one of the "wheels of trade" that helps produce an international economy. In the same way, Ishmael's representation of whaling and the international economy as a site of universal and transcendent identities and relations does not quite "empty the decanter" of this real economy, for it also renders this inventory as a coherent mercantile system of individual, national, and international positions. Ishmael's metaphysical nominalization of the real is not unlike the mercantilist discourse that conceptualizes all economic activity as a single, all-encompassing system of economic meaning.

"The Decanter" demonstrates a pattern in *Moby Dick* by which the people, places, and practices of whaling are rendered in a vision that tends to represent differences (e.g., national propensities) in order to liquidate them in the transcendent try-works of a common humanity and a discursive coop of metaphysical universals. Yet as with Ishmael's mercantile tally of Dan Coopman's log, this unifying vision oils the wheels of trade as much as it dissolves them, for the Pequod is not only a kind of domestic household within the international economy, but also a version of this international economy rendered *as* domestic household, a metaphor that is itself the condition for realizing the more universal and transcendent possibilities of exchange. And just as Smith deploys the colonial discourse to articulate this possibility, so too does *Moby Dick*.

We can trace this discourse by first seeing how Melville formulates the world as an economic configuration, then delineates these economic identities and relations in terms of colonial exchange. Before signing on with a ship, Ishmael asks "Who ain't a slave?" and suggests that this economic predicament can be apprehended "either in a physical or metaphysical point of view" as he speaks of both the "thump and punch" dealt by sea-captains and the "universal thump" felt by all men (25). Moreover, this thump delineates everybody's position in expressly financial terms:

> they make a point of paying me for my trouble, whereas they never pay passengers a single penny . . . . On the contrary, passengers must pay. And there is all the difference in the world between paying and being paid. The act of paying is perhaps the most uncomfortable infliction that the two orchard thieves entailed upon us. But being paid—what will compare with it? (25)

Ishmael's economic configuration of the world, as well as his particular account of a single whaling venture, is critically shaped by colonial encounter, in which his own psychological and economic disequilibrium is first resolved in terms of his establishment in a relationship with Queequeg. This relationship is depicted both as an exchange in the international marketplace and as the realization of a domestic household. This joint-production is more fully played out on board the Pequod, in which the male sphere of economic production also suggests an engendered and self-contained space that is as much domestic household (including its representation as a site of consumption) as working factory. The creation of economic wealth on the Pequod involves imagining the ship not only as a microeconomic site of production, but also as an entire international economy rendered as a unified and domesticated system of production, exchange, and consumption.

Ishmael explains his decision to go whaling partly in terms of economics: "having little or no money in my purse," he tells us, he decides to "see the watery part of the world" (23). Yet this economic lack is something of an alibi, since the more critical disequilibrium would seem to lie in Ishmael's need for "driving off the spleen and regulating the circulation." "[G]rowing grim about the mouth," "involuntarily pausing before coffin warehouses, and bringing up the rear of every funeral," Ishmael feels his "hypos" getting an "upper hand," and taking to a ship is his notion of something more than just an economic resolution. Ishmael's encounter with Queequeg is also the result of a series of predicaments and choices nominally tied to economic conditions. For example, his store of funds dictates his choice of lodging in New Bedford: "my dear Ishmael, be sure to inquire the price, and don't be too particular" (27). Ishmael therefore finds himself at the Spouter-Inn, where again a scarcity of funds and options determines his fate—only a bench or a shared bed with a "dark-complexioned" harpooner (32), whose uncertain identity precipitates a series of exchanges between Ishmael and Peter Coffin. In this instance, economic constraint is tied to a dread of the colonial other specifically signified in the practice of cannibalism, even as the identity of the practitioner remains unclear. Moreover, economic enterprise and colonial encounter are further conjoined in the absence of the cannibal, who is busy at the "cannibal business" of selling heads. As Coffin toys with Ishmael, market discourse and colonialist dread toy with each other:

> "That's precisely it," said the landlord, "and I told him he couldn't sell it here, the market's overstocked."
>
> "With what?" shouted I.
>
> "With heads, to be sure; ain't there too many heads in the world?"
>
> "I tell you what it is, landlord," said I, quite calmly, "you'd better stop spinning that yarn to me—I'm not green."
>
> "May be not . . . but I rayther guess you'll be done *brown* if that ere harpooner hears you a slanderin' his head."
>
> "I'll break it for him," said I, now flying into a passion again at this unaccountable farrago of the landlord's.
>
> "It's broke a'ready," said he.
>
> "Broke said I—'*broke* do you mean?" (35)

At this point Ishmael doesn't know whether his bed-partner is white or not, although he earlier admits that he "began to feel suspicious of this 'dark complexioned' harpooner" (32). Again, Ishmael seeks to clarify the nature of the activity of the stranger, in which market madness is linked to primitive practice:

> "I now demand of you to speak out and tell me who and what this harpooner is . . . . you will be so good as to unsay that story about selling his head, which if true I take to be good evidence that this harpooner is stark mad, and I've no idea of sleeping with a madman." (35)

This confusion about the identity of the harpooner sets up the encounter scene between Ishmael and Queequeg, for when Ishmael sees the stranger's tattooed face for the first time, the image presents Ishmael with both the dread of a colonial encounter of difference and a reflexive encounter with another white man mutilated by cannibals:

> I remembered the story of a white man—a whaleman too—who, falling among the cannibals, had been tattooed by them. I concluded that this harpooneer, in the course of his distant voyages, must have met with a similar adventure. And what is it, thought I, after all! It's only his outside; a man can be honest in any sort of skin. (37)

Ishmael can comfort himself because he can read difference as sameness; however, his unease continues as he seeks to account for the stranger's darkness and other signs of difference. As the stranger continues to undress, Ishmael's terror grows, until the appearance of the wooden idol convinces him that this strange "peddler of heads" must indeed be a "heathen" and an "abominable savage" (38). Queequeg jumps into bed with the tomahawk pipe, Ishmael cries out, Coffin rushes in to mediate the dispute, and Ishmael eventually falls in bed with Queequeg for the best sleep of his life (40).

The next morning, Ishmael awakens to Queequeg's "loving and affectionate" embrace, in which Ishmael feels like a wife in Queequeg's "bridegroom clasp" (40-1). The sexual imagery is indeed complicated, a "counterpane" mosaic of dirty transgression (the memory of crawling up the chimney), substitute-maternal punishment (the stepmother's bedroom banishment), mysterious touching (the "shock" of the unseen "supernatural hand"), and phallic transformation (the violent threat of the tomahawk socialized as peace-pipe). However we might wish to interpret such intimacies, these engendered configurations serve to bring Queequeg back into circulation in the domestic economy, for although still an "undergraduate," he is at least in some "small degree civilized," as his morning toiletries attest. In the same way, a series of economic tropes and real exchanges further this domestication.

First, Ishmael's sense of the joke played on him by Coffin is rendered in terms of economic exchange: "So, if any one man, in his own proper person, afford stuff for a good joke to anybody, let him not be backward, but let him cheerfully allow himself to spend and be spent in that way" (43). Furthermore, once Ishmael experiences the "melting" of his resistances to Queequeg and decides to "try a pagan friend" (59), a series of exchanges ensue: they share a book, a social smoke, conversation, and physical embrace, all of which results in Queequeg's telling Ishmael that they are "married." Later Queequeg gives Ishmael both the embalmed head and fifteen dollars in silver. Ishmael says, "I was going to remonstrate; but he silenced me by pouring them into my trousers' pockets. I let them stay" (59-60). The currency of "bosom" friendship (57), in turn, circulates into the wider economy when Ishmael settles both his and Queequeg's lodging bill by using the money given to him (63).

Both this domestic arrangement and its delineation in terms of international economy continue to develop in the chapters depicting the growth of their friendship, its registration in ever-widening social spheres, and their signing on with the Pequod. Ishmael's "melting" heart liquidates social references, cultural differences, and economic positions in a metaphysical discourse of universal identities and transcendent relations. For example, in "Bosom Friend" (Chapter 10), Ishmael likens Queequeg's pagan visage to "General Washington's head, as seen in the popular busts of him," and suggests that "Queequeg was George Washington, cannibalistically developed" (58), thereby placing Queequeg (something like a dollar bill) in circulation in a domestic economy of American signification. In the next chapter ("Nightgown") Ishmael and Queequeg lie in bed, and this colonial exchange is rendered in terms of warmth and cold, in which all identities are produced in a system of differences: "to enjoy bodily warmth, some small part of you must be cold, for there is no quality in this world that is not what it is merely by contrast. Nothing exists in itself" (61). With regard to Queequeg, Ishmael's attempts to "melt" difference resemble the monetization of real differences in a universalizing system of value, which, in turn, has ramifications for their active participation in—and production of—an international economy.

Accordingly, this personal exchange is quickly widened into what Ishmael interprets as Queequeg's self-representation as a member of a "mutual, joint-stock world, in all meridians" (67) as they conduct the display of their friendship in a series of widening social spheres—from bedroom to breakfast room to New Bedford streets, and then on board the Moss on its way to Nantucket, where they seek their lays on board the Pequod. In "The Ship" (Chapter 16) the Pequod both literally and symbolically delineates the world as a system of economic identities and relations. While Captain Peleg differentiates "Marchant service" from whaling (73), the latter is not so much outside the realm of economic activity as it is a mercantilist venture more centrally tied to the creation of real wealth. Moreover, when Ishmael insists that he wants "to see what whaling is. I want to see the world," Peleg points him toward "the open ocean," an "exceedingly monotonous and forbidding" prospect of "nothing but water" with not "the slightest variety" (73-5). "Can't ye see the world where you stand?" Peleg asks. In the world of whaling, every place is the same place, an obstensibly isolationist or protectionist view that nevertheless imagines a single world "girdled with guineas" and organized entirely in terms of the "universal thump" of economic production, payments, and dividends.

Yet the Pequod is not just a site of economic production, for it also suggests a self-contained economy of production and consumption in which international identities and relations (again largely configured in terms of colonial encounter) are rendered as a domestic household. Between the first whale kill in Chapter 61 ("Stubb Kills a Whale") and the long meditation on the doubloon in Chapter 99 (The Doubloon"), we're given something like a dissection of the economic processes of market production and consumption: natural resources are secured, various production processes and technologies are employed to effect the conversion from primary resource to semi-manufactured commodity, storage and distribution mechanisms are in place, and various sorts of capital and consumer consumption sustain both production and leisure. However, in this staging of the economic process, the conventional distinctions between production and consumption are destabilized: the male sphere of marketplace production is rendered as a gendered domestic household, just as the "factory output" is itself consumed in part by its own producers. This representation of the Pequod as both a domestic household and a site of international economy is a way of imagining international economy as a single household.

The economic enterprise of whaling is organized around the body of the whale, and in this sense the production of wealth in *Moby Dick* is crucially linked to "real" material conditions.[10] This aspect underscores how the merely monetary nominalizations of the doubloon—what makes the coin "so killing wonderful"—take us beyond the abstractions of representation: "the whale once more rolled out into view; surging from side to side; spasmodically dilating and contracting his spout-hole, with sharp, cracking, agonized respirations. At last, gush after gush of clotted red gore . . . shot into the frighted air . . . . His heart had burst!" When Daggoo announces, "He's dead Mr. Stubb," Stubb notes, "Yes; both pipes out," then takes his pipe out of his mouth and "scattered the dead ashes over the water; and, for a moment, stood thoughtfully eyeing the vast corpse he had made" (230).

Like Ishmael's personal identity and relations, this economic process, with its emphasis on real conditions, is importantly linked to the figurations of a primitive other. In "Stubb's Supper" (Chapter 64) the distinction between the spheres of production and consumption is partly erased when Stubb calls for a steak cut from the whale he's killed:

> Here be it known, that though these wild fishermen do not as a general thing, and according to the great military maxim, make the enemy defray the current expenses of the war (at least before realizing the proceeds of the voyage), yet now and then you find some of these Nantucketeers who have a genuine relish for that particular part . . . designated by Stubb. (234)

This first scene of consumption in the economic process is embedded figuratively in a number of images of colonialist encounter. First, while feeding on the corpse in the water, the sharks are "longingly gazing up" through the "smoking horror and diabolism" to the "table where red meat is being carved" and are "ready to bolt down every killed man that is tossed to them" (234). Furthermore, the image of shark and man is a reflexive equation that links cannibalism and slavery:

> while the valiant butchers over the deck-table are thus cannibally carving each other's live meat with carving-knives all gilded and tasselled, the sharks, also, with the jewel-hilted mouths, are quarrelsomely carving away . . . were you to turn the whole affair upside down, it would still be pretty much the same thing . . . a shocking sharkish business enough for all parties . . . . sharks are the invariable outriders of all slave ships crossing the Atlantic, systemically trotting alongside, to be handy in case a parcel is to be carried anywhere, or a deal slave to be decently buried. (234-5)

In addition to cannibalism and slavery, Stubb's supper stages a third aspect of colonial encounter, the missionary exhortations to the sharks by the black cook Fleece, who functions as a kind of ventriloquist's dummy for Stubb:

> "What a shindy they are kicking up! Cook, go and talk to 'em; tell 'em they are welcome to help themselves civilly . . . but they must keep quiet. Blast me, if I can hear my own voice. Away, cook, and deliver my message. Here, take this lantern . . . now then, go and preach to 'em!" (235)

Fleece's name and position suggests both Christian imagery and the swindle implicit in the entire exchange, insofar as he is the black sheep who has been trained by Stubb to cook the white man's cannibalistic object of desire raw.

The relationship between production and consumption, like the depiction of colonial encounter, is rendered in a system that brings different economic spheres into exchange in such a way as to undermine conventional distinctions. For example, in the next chapter, "The Whale as a Dish" (Chapter 65), Ishmael ponders this relation: "That mortal man should feed upon the creature that feeds his lamps, and, like Stubb, eat him by his own light, as you may say; this seems so outlandish a thing that one must needs go a little into the history and philosophy of it" (238). However, this "outlandish" occurrence is rendered palatable by locating it within the familiar economic analysis of the relation between scarcity and value, which again is organized around the distinction between civilized and uncivilized sensibilities. First, Ishmael justifies the eating of whale meat by arguing that it has been a "delicacy" and has commanded large prices in France (238). However, since luxury goods sustain their value partly by virtue of their scarcity, whale meat would seem to violate this criterion of value for whalers: "The fact is, that among the hunters at least, the whale would by all hands be considered a noble dish, were there not so much of him; but when you come to sit down before a meat-pie nearly one hundred feet long, it takes away your appetite" (239). Only primitives (Esquimaux), survivalists (English whalers abandoned in Greenland), and "the most unprejudiced of men" (like Stubb) appreciate the whale meat. Ishmael then offers another explanation for "what further depreciates the whale as a civilized dish . . . his exceeding richness," yet casts off the explanation just as quickly to return to the initial problem of production by way of consumption:

> It is not, perhaps, entirely because the whale is so excessively unctuous that landsmen seem to regard the eating of him with abhorrence; that appears to result, in some way, from the consideration before mentioned; i.e. that a man should eat a newly murdered thing of the sea, and eat it by its own light. (239-240)

This relation between production and consumption is seen with "abhorrence" precisely because it is so visible, a connection that is usually hidden in the "meatmarket of a Saturday night." Again, this entire query is configured in terms of the colonialist encounter of cannibalism: "Does not that sight take a tooth out of the cannibal's jaw? Cannibals? who is not a cannibal?" Finally, this reflexive equation between civilized and primitive consumption is cast as an economic distinction between primary needs and luxurious excess: "I tell you it will be more tolerable for the Fejee, I say, in the day of judgment, than for thee, civilized and enlightened gourmand, who nailest geese to the ground and feastest on their bloated livers in thy paté-de-foie-gras" (240).

Repeatedly, the economic narrative of production and consumption is marked by configurations of colonial encounter: First, the cannibalistic sharks, "wedder [created by] Fejee god or Nantucket god," must be massacred to make possible the whalers' own meat consumption (240). Second, the markings in the blubber blanket "afford the ground for . . . delineations . . . hieroglyphical; that is, if you call those mysterious cyphers on the walls of pyramids hieroglyphics, then that is the proper word to use in the present connexion," thereby suggesting not only an Orientalist reference to Egypt, but also "the old Indian characters chiselled on the famous hieroglyphic palisades on the banks of the Upper Mississippi" (244). Third, the decapitated whale is rendered as "a black and hooded head . . . [that] hanging there . . . seemed the Sphynx's in the desert" (247), to which Ahab speaks as did Oedipus, although Ahab cannot solve the riddle ("not one syllable is thine!"). The image of the Sphynx calls forth not only the ancient Greek narrative, but also the Egyptian figure Ra, the sun-god ("I'd strike the sun if it insulted me"). Fourth, Ishmael describes his connection to Queequeg by means of the monkey-rope as analogous to "Italian organ-boys holding a dancing ape by a long cord" (253), and so "this Siamese connexion" of their joint-enterprise is specifically grounded in an equation of racial difference and identity.

The encounter with the Rose-bud suggests another particular kind of consumption as a source of economic production, and the exchange is also imperialist and sexual in its figuration. First, Stubb "diddles" the French (the female rose-bud) in the imperialist competition for exploitation of the seas. After the ship is on its way, Stubb digs into the rotten corpse in such a way as to recall a kind of inverted narrative of imperialist origins: "it was like turning up old Roman tiles and pottery buried in fat English loam" (316). Once again, production (extracting the ambergris) is marked by death and the rot of consumption, and the two realms are fluid and ultimately conflated: "suddenly from out the very heart of this plague, there stole a faint stream of perfume, which flowed through the tide of bad smells without being absorbed by it, as one river will flow into and then along with another, without at all blending with it for a time" (316).

Ambergris connects economic luxury ("perfumery, pastiles, precious candles, hair-powders, and pomatum") with "the inglorious bowels of a sick whale" (317). Ishmael pursues this apparent incongruity to "repel a charge often made against whalemen . . . . the slanderous aspersion . . . that the vocation of whaling is a slatternly, untidy business" (318). He goes on to distinguish the unfinished rotting oil first brought to London by Greenland whaling ships from those that "try" the oil as do the Southern ships, which render and purify the oil until it is "nearly scentless," and the juxtaposition between this insistence and the account of the ambergris would suggest something like a concern over a "sexual stink." Furthermore, he likens the scent and activity of the whale to the gesture of the female in the domestic household: "I say, that the motion of a Sperm Whale's flukes above water dispenses a perfume, as when a musk-scented lady rustles her dress in a warm parlor" (318-9). Ambergris therefore suggests a connection between production and consumption as an image of an economic resource produced from biological decay, as well as a reconfiguration of the gendered distinction between productive and consumptive sites of economic exchange: the floating factory is also household parlor. Likewise, "Cisterns and Buckets" (Chapter 78) suggests a gendered connection between economic activity and colonialism, for just as whaling is likened to an originary "Egyptian mother," so too does the extraction of the purest spermaceti from the whale head involve the the primitive "obstetrics of Queequeg, the deliverance, or rather delivery of Tashtego" (270). The lesson that this "primitive detour" provides Ishmael is that the female sphere of "Midwifery should be taught in the same course with fencing and boxing, riding and rowing."

These gendered links conjoining economic activity and colonial exchange are perhaps most evident in the three chapters that precede "The Doubloon"—"The Try-works," "The Lamp," and "Stowing Down and Clearing Up" (Chapters 96-8). The process is begun with the initial stoking of the furnace by wood, after which the burning of the whale recalls the solipsistic obsessions of Ahab, the all-consuming metaphysics of Ishmael, and colonial encounter:

> Like a plethoric burning martyr, or a self-consuming misanthrope, once ignited, the whale supplies his own fuel and burns by his own body. Would that he consumed his own smoke! for his smoke his horrible to inhale, and inhale it you must, and not only that, but you must live in it for the time. It has an unspeakable, wild, Hindoo odor about it. (326)

And once the works are in full operation, the scene turns into a kind of cannibalistic nightmare of unworldly terror:

> the Tartarean shapes of the pagan harpooners . . . . pitched hissing masses of blubber into the scalding pots, or stirred up the fires underneath . . . . tawny features, now all begrimed with smoke and sweat, their matted beards, and the contrasting barbaric brilliancy of their teeth . . . . they narrated to each other their unholy adventures, their tales of terror . . . their uncivilized laughter forked upwards out of them, like the flames from the furnace . . . the harpooners wildly gesticulated with their huge pronged forks and dippers; as the wind howled on, and the sea leaped, and the ship groaned and dived, and yet steadfastly shot her red hell further and further into the blackness of the sea and the night, and scornfully champed the white bone in her mouth, and viciously spat round her on all sides; then the rushing Pequod, freighted with savages, and laden with fire, and burning a corpse, and plunging into that blackness of darkness, seemed material counterpart of her monomaniac commander's soul. (327)

The conflation of the economic enterprise and cannibalistic nightmare casts Ishmael, who is at the tiller of the ship, into an "unnatural hallucination of the night" in which the compass points are reversed and distinctions dissolved:

> I was horribly conscious of something fatally wrong. . . . I thought my eyes were open . . . . But, spite of all this, I could see no compass . . . . A stark, bewildered feeling, as of death, came over me. Convulsively, my hands grasped the tiller, but with the crazy conceit that the tiller was, somehow, in some enchanted way, inverted. (328)

"The Try-works" ends with Ishmael's rendering of events into philosophical meditation, much as the next two chapters render the whale to oil. Accordingly, in "The Lamp" Ishmael notes how merchant seamen labor in the dark, whereas whaling seamen enjoy an abundance of oil, an observation that implicitly conjoins the economic activities of the production and consumption of the whale with loftier illumination:

> See with what entire freedom the whaleman takes his handful of lamps . . . to the copper cooler at the try-works, and replenishes them there, as mugs of ale at a vat. He burns, too, the purest of oil, in its unmanufactured, and, therefore, invitiated state; a fluid unknown to . . . contrivances ashore. . . . He goes and hunts for his oil, so as to be sure of its freshness and genuineness, even as the traveller on the prairie hunts up his own supper of game. (329)

Finally, before the meditation of the doubloon, the ship is converted into a gendered domestic household. In "Stowing Down and Clearing Up" (Chapter 98), Ishmael reviews the stages of sighting, chasing, slaughtering, and rendering into pots:

> but now it remains to conclude the last chapter of this part of the description by rehearsing—singing, if I may—the romantic proceeding of decanting off his oil into the casks and striking them down into the hold, where once again leviathan returns to his native profundities, sliding along beneath the surface as before; but alas! never more to rise and blow. (330)

He then describes the casking, after which "the bowels of the ship are thrown open, and down go the casks to their final rest at sea. This done, the hatches are replaced, and hermetically closed, like a closet walled up" (330).

While this passage can be read as foreshadowing of the sinking of the Pequod, it also resembles the economic self-containment of the ship: all production and consumption are complete and self-contained. This is why the next paragraph explores "one of the most remarkable incidents in all of the business of whaling": how the economic carnage is erased by both the "singular cleansing virtue" of the oil and the domestic hygiene of the ship's hands who "diligently . . . restore" the ship to "full tidiness." After all evidence is either cleaned or hidden from view, "the crew themselves proceed to their own ablutions . . . and finally issue from the immaculate deck, fresh and all aglow, as bridegrooms" (330). Or, rather, as brides and grooms, for the domestic scene is complete: "Now, with elated steps, they pace the planks in two and threes, and humorously discourse of parlors, sofas, carpets, and fine cambrices; propose to mat the deck; think of having hangins to the top; object not to taking tea by moonlight on the piazza of the forecastle" (331). Finally, the closure is underscored by the repetition of the entire process:

> when . . . they have finally bestirred themselves to cleanse the ship . . . many is the time the poor fellows, just buttoning the necks of their clean frocks, are startled by the cry of "There she blows!" and away they fly to fight another whale, and go through the whole weary thing again. Oh! my friends, this is man-killing! Yet this is life. (331)

By rendering the Pequod as a site of economic production and consumption, Melville represents it as a kind of self-contained domestic household and as the possibility of an international economy brought under one unified roof, which facilitates both literal economic exchange and the metaphysical transactions of this universalizing and transcendent fictional economy. And as has been shown, these representations and realities are crucially linked to the colonial discourse that both delineates exchange values and negotiates them in a single working system. The colonial is, as it were, the currency upon which these values are inscribed. Accordingly, the doubloon is itself inscribed with a colonial discourse insofar as it suggests a variety of Orientalist figurations of the exotic other, and it is the monetization of this inscription that enables the doubloon to do its representational work as a "killing wonderful" agent of signification.

The doubloon, like the gold of which it is made, operates in *Moby Dick* as a general equivalent by which many identities and relations are represented. For the characters in the novel the doubloon is a secured signifier nailed to the masthead of the ship, yet it floats in a reflective sea of subjective positions. Perhaps in the doubloon Melville is offering us a paradoxical meditation on gold as a standard, for even this universal measure and store of value, upon which all eyes gaze, is itself subjectively and polymorphously melted down and recast in the fiat image of each man. Yet the coin's representational capacities as a signifier of value are not tied so much to the gold of which it is made, as to the text inscribed upon it. As Ahab puts it while gazing at "this equatorial coin": "There's something ever egotistical . . . . all are Ahab; and this round gold is but the image of the roundabout globe, which, like a magician's glass, to each and every man in turn but mirrors back his own mysterious self" (333). In the same way, the entire chapter of "The Doubloon" presents a series of subjective queries as to the meaning or value of the coin that render all participants in a unified system whereby differences are freely circulated and exchanged.

Stubb begins by asserting that unlike Ahab and Starbuck, who gaze into the coin as a symbol, he would "not look at it very long ere spending it" (333). Stubb finds this sort of metaphysical inquiry "queer." He next suggests that it is not the gold itself but the inscriptions on it that apparently make the doubloon "so killing wonderful," for he has seen similar gold doubloons of many nations that lack this attraction. His curiosity raised, he proceeds to examine the "signs and wonders" inscribed upon the coin in order to "try [his] hand at raising a meaning out of these queer curvicues"

(333). Yet like all "books [that] must know [their] places," the "almanack" that Stubb uses as his guide for interpreting the coin can only "give us the bare words and facts, but we come in to supply the thoughts" (334).

Stubb tries to work out its meaning himself, then continues the inquiry as a sort of narrative conductor, as he hides behind the try-works, listens to the thoughts of others, and offers comment. Flask, for example, sees only a "round thing made of gold" and notes that "whoever raises a certain whale, this round thing belongs to him" (334). The gold coin means nothing except "sixteen dollars . . . and at two cents the cigar, that's nine hundred and sixty cigars." For Flask, the gold and its configuration as specie are a store and measure of value that represents only the exchange value of real commodities. Stubb cannot decide whether to "call that wise or foolish." The Manxman offers another interpretation, and again Stubb notes, "There's another rendering now; but still one text." When Queequeg approaches, Stubb notes the similarity between the inscriptions on the coin and those on Queequeg's body, as if subject and object are "comparing notes." This link recalls Ahab's solipsism ("All are Ahab"), yet configures that specular relation as a monetary trope of colonial encounter.

Finally, Pip's response—"I look, you look, he looks; we look, ye look, they look"—suggests for Stubb the connections between language ("Murray's Grammar"), money, and meaning. Stubb leaves Pip to his "muttering" meaning-making, who then proceeds to offer a complicated interpretation of gold as the general equivalent, the reflective "eye" at the center of the ship: "Here's the ship's navel, this doubloon here, and they are all fit to unscrew it. But, unscrew your navel, and what's the consequence?" Yet for Pip there is something "ugly" and "desperate" in the coin remaining bound to the mast, like "some old darkey's wedding ring" hidden inside the rings of a pine tree. Similarly, Pip fears that the sea is the "green miser" that will soon hoard the "precious, precious gold." Pip's prophecy, like the entire series of interpretations, entails a number of suggestive monetary tropes: gold as the center of a system, the consequences of the circulation and hoarding of gold, the coin as a signifier of racial identity and difference, and even the ocean as a green text backed by gold reserves.

As already noted, in a novel so given over to the production of signification, meaning, and value, the monetary configurations of the gold doubloon are indeed suggestive. To repeat the point made in regard to the relation between Ishmael and Queequeg, Pip's observation about the coin-as-navel recalls Ahab's tendency to see the coin as both self-reflective eye and connecting link to the whole world, and this monetary metaphysics is specifically represented in Orientalist configurations of the primitive and exotic literally written into the gold. Although the coin is actually Ecuadorean, it is rendered as something much more imaginary than any single place on a real map. First, the doubloon is filled with exotic glyphs: "[Ahab] seemed to be newly attracted by the strange figures and inscriptions stamped on it" (332). Second, this exoticism speaks to the Orientalist search for origins and the narratives of Edenic abundance and innocence: "Now this doubloon was of the purest, virgin gold, raked somewhere out of the heart of gorgeous hills, whence, east and west, over golden sands, the head-waters of many a Pactolus flows" (332). Third, this exotic narrative of origins is inscrutable, a magical picture that cannot speak: "those noble golden coins of South America are as medals of the sun and tropic token-pieces. Here palms, alpacas, and volcanoes; sun's disks and stars, ecliptics, horns-of-plenty, and rich banners waving, are in luxuriant profusion stamped" and "the signs [are] all marked with their usual cabalistics" (332). Fourth, the material purity of the doubloon, insulated from history, is juxtaposed with the historical registrations of the west:

> nailed amidst all the rustiness of iron bolts and the verdigris of copper spikes, yet, untouchable and immaculate to any foulness, it still preserved its Quito glow. . . . For it was set apart and sanctified to one awe-striking end . . . . this bright coin came from a country planted in the middle of the world . . . it had been cast . . . in the unwaning clime that knows no autumn. (332)

Finally, the doubloon poses a link, albeit an oppositional one, between metaphysical meaning and the business of buying and selling:

> for the first time [Ahab was] beginning to interpret for himself in some monomaniac way whatever significance lurks in all things, else all things are little worth, and the round world itself but an empty cipher, except to sell by the cartload . . . to fill up some morass in the Milky Way. (332)

Ahab's gaze resembles Lacan's Oedipal configuration of the Imaginary, in which the self gazes at the world and sees only a reflection of self, as if still tied to the mother/other by an uncut cord. This Oedipal configuration, as reflected in the coin, is also Orientalist in its inflection, just as Ishmael makes a similar claim about his relation with Queequeg and even whaling itself: "whaling may well be regarded as that Egyptian mother, who bore offspring themselves pregnant from her womb" (100).

The representation of the doubloon, like whaling as the discursive cord conjoining everything in the world in *Moby Dick*, suggests how money entails a link between all romantic meaning-making and the realization of an economic system. Similarly, this realization is configured by way of a colonial discourse that is itself monetized, in the sense that it affords the nominalization of an array of identities and differences, and then brings them under the one roof of a worldwide domestic household—a free-trade romance nominalized as a vision of universal exchange and transcendent values far beyond the real conditions rendered there. The long-standing debate about the neutrality of money offers a strategy for exploring the relationship between representation and reality in *Moby Dick* in terms of novel's own reserves of monetary figuration and real economic subject matter. Melville's novel is a fictional nominalization of whaling that, like money, oils the wheels of trade, and in doing so, takes its own turn in the realization of international economy.

NOTES

[1] Throughout this chapter, I am using the term "Orientalism" rather loosely to denote those discursive formations by which the West has represented the non-Western "other." Edward Said's use of the term in *Orientalism* refers not only to the disciplinary study of the Orient in particular, but also to a broader constellation of Western practices, beliefs, and attitudes variously linked with colonial imperialism.

[2] For a wide selection of essays addressing money and American fiction, see Roy R. Male. ed., *Money Talks: Language and Lucre in American Fiction.*

[3] See, for example, Carlo Cipolla, *Money, Prices, and Civilization in the Mediterranean World: Fifth to Seventeenth Century*, and Peter H. Ramsey, ed., *The Price Revolution in Sixteenth Century England.*

[4] Jean Bodin's 1568 analysis of the price revolution and his observation of the relationship between money supply and prices is sometimes given credit as the "discovery" of the quantity theory of money. See, for example, Joseph Schumpeter's discussion of early quantity theory in *The History of Economic Analysis*, 311-7.

[5] For a short standard overview of mercantilist doctrine and practice, see Robert B. Ekelund, Jr. and Robert F. Hebert, *A History of Economic Theory and Method* (42-71). It is important to emphasize that distinctions between doctrine and practice, the range of views within mercantilist discourse, and post-mercantilist interpretations of those views make for a much more complicated story. See also Joseph A. Schumpeter's discussion in *History of Economic Analysis*, 276-378, for a more extensive and problematic treatment from an economist's perspective. Similarly, In *The Order of Things: An Archeology of the Human Sciences*, Michel Foucault challenges conventional economic readings of mercantilism in his analysis of representation in various discourses of this period. See pp. 166-216.

[6] The law of comparative advantage says that even where one country or economic agent can more effectively produce all goods than another, it should produce only those goods where its advantage is greatest. If I am better than you at both regular whaling and white whaling, I should go after the whale that brings me the greatest relative returns, and leave the other to you.

[7] For similar readings of Ahab's economic quest, see Charles Olsón, *Call Me Ishmael*, and Paul Rogin, *Subversive Genealogy: The Politics and Art of Herman Melville*. Moreover, instead of reading Ahab as looking for new areas of industrial production, we might see how he points to both an anxiety about and a solution beyond this phase of capitalism, one in which there is "no more place to go." For example, it can be somewhat surprising to the contemporary reader to encounter so many clues about the anxiety of economic coverage and exhaustion in mid-nineteenth century—the whaling adventure is from the beginning rendered as something like nostalgia and decay (old whaling stories, the markers of dead sailors in the church, tired ships), swimming holes are fished out, markets have been forced to relocate (Nantucket to New Bedford), and the globe is already entirely inscribed and domesticated by economic exchange ("girdled by guineas"). Ahab's radical turn "inward," rather than being a turning away from the economic imagination, might instead be a turn to another kind of economic pursuit, in which new markets are created and exploited.

[8] Thornton argued that an increase in the money supply would tend to increase savings, a part of which could be used by entrepreneurs as capital investment, which, in turn, would affect output. Mill noted that a strict connection between money supply and prices was more problematic in an economy in which credit comes into play.

[9] Indeed, the concept of national accounting is itself a key mercantilist development. Consider the "political arithemetick" of William Petty: "The Method I take . . . , is not very usual; for instead of using only comparative and superlative words, and intellectual Arguments, I have taken the course (as a Specimen of

the Political Arithmetick I have long aimed at) to express myself in Terms of Number, Weight, or Measure; to use only Arguments of Sense, and to consider only such Causes, as have visible Foundations in Nature." *The Economic Writings of Sir William Petty*, 244 (qtd. in Ekelund, 74).

[10] *Moby Dick* could therefore be read in light of what Michel Foucault's described as a difference between pre-classical analyses of wealth, with its emphasis on money and representation, and classical political economy, with its focus on a more historicized discourse of labor, production, and death. (See *The Order of Things*, Chapters 6-8.)

CHAPTER 5

Desire and Indifference in *Sister Carrie*

Neoclassical Economic Anticipations

> *"if we can compare the quantities . . . we do not need the units."*
>
> —WILLIAM STANLEY JEVONS, *THE THEORY OF POLITICAL ECONOMY*

> *"there are only differences, without positive terms."*
>
> —FERDINAND DE SAUSSURE, *COURSE IN GENERAL LINGUISTICS*

Sister Carrie is a naturalist melodrama in which the economy plays a leading role. What F. O. Mathiessen referred to as Theodore Dreiser's "picture of conditions" is a novelistic representation of American capitalism toward the end of the nineteenth century, with extensive descriptions of department stores and working conditions, conspicuous consumption and grinding poverty, and individual desire and class conflict. This naturalist picture of economic conditions, however, is not a distant painterly backdrop for the story of Carrie Meeber and George Hurstwood, but is instead an important thematic and dramatic element of the novel, as is suggested in Carrie's definition of money: "something everybody else has and I must get," an equation in which Carrie's desire is specifically configured as an economic problem (54). Similarly, Hurstwood's economic decline from a middle-class saloon manager to a streetcar scab and then to an unemployed and homeless suicide exemplifies how a character's place in the economy significantly registers his or her position in the fiction.

Economic identities and relations are crucial to Dreiser's many representations of desire, such as sexual drive, the longing for fame, or the exhibitionist wish to be seen as spectacle. We might even take as our trope for reading this relation between desire and economics in *Sister Carrie* the character Drouet, the travelling salesman whose "drumming" is no more confined to a single place of business than it is limited to strictly economic concerns, and for whom the marketplace is, as it were, every place. In his first encounter with Carrie, Drouet is described as both a "drummer" and a "masher" whose "dress and manners" link his performance as a salesman to his amorous appeal for Carrie (7). Drouet's skills as a salesman are initially described in terms of his exchanges with women in places of business such as department stores in which the "sale" involves not merchandise but sexual conquest, for Drouet's mind is "actuated not by greed, but an insatiable love of variable pleasure. His method was always simple. Its principal element was daring, backed, of course, by an intense desire and admiration for the sex" (8).

Indeed, Dreiser's pronounced concern with desire in all its configurations has led critics to address it as a key element of the novel, even, as Lawrence Hussman has suggestively described it, as the "protagonist of *Sister Carrie*" (18). Accordingly, I wish to explore two related areas of critical neglect regarding Dreiser's representation of desire and its relation to his economic subject matter. The first one involves Dreiser's representation of "indifference" in *Sister Carrie*. Critics have given little thought to Dreiser's use of the concept of "indifference," which is crucial to an understanding of how desire is structured and sustained in *Sister Carrie*. Explicit references to indifference appear in the novel more than fifty times, yet readers have not addressed Dreiser's deployment of indifference as a naturalist trope that informs the novel's rhetorical and figurative operations, organizes its narrative structure and use of point of view, and delineates dramatic exchanges among his characters. The variety and pervasiveness of Dreiser's use of indifference in his representation of desire in the fictional economy of *Sister Carrie* suggests that the relationship between desire and indifference is much more extensive and complex than critics have allowed. Critics either ignore indifference or—more importantly—gloss it in terms of some binary opposition to, or absence of, desire. In my reading of indifference in *Sister Carrie*, I wish to explore a more fluid, dynamic, and problematic exchange between desire and indifference, as well as to argue that it constitutes a key element of *Sister Carrie*'s naturalist economy, by which I mean the economic conditions and the novelistic means by which Dreiser produces them.

The other area of critical oversight involves the absence of any discussion of neoclassical economic theory (specifically its use of marginal utility analysis), whose emergence toward the end of the nineteenth century and whose analysis of individual desire, economic consumption, and market outcome point to suggestive historical and thematic coincidences with Dreiser's fiction. While I do not argue that the novel can be read as an exact mimetic performance of neoclassical utility theory, this widely overlooked economic model provides a useful point of reference for reconsidering the representation of desire in *Sister Carrie*, especially insofar as it variously anticipates, corroborates, and challenges key aspects of contemporary poststructuralist readings of desire that make reference to economic concepts and conditions.

Readers have often linked economics to other aspects of novelistic form and technique in *Sister Carrie*, such as its structure, point of view, and linguistic style. Perhaps the most commonly cited connection between economic subject matter and plot structure involves Carrie's rise and Hurstwood's fall, in which narrative equilibrium is a function of economic conditions.[1] In addition to novelistic structure, Dreiser's use of point of view and his language have been addressed by critics in terms of economics. Fredric Jameson, for example, has argued for a connection between capitalist conditions and Dreiser's modernist "construction of the subject" as "a closed monad," in which the technique of point of view reifies desire as "merely psychological experience, private feeling, or relativized value" (160). Jameson also gives a Marxist interpretation of the often-noted "difficulties" of Dreiser's style, arguing that the "paradox about Dreiser—he is best at his worst—is peculiarly intensified by the problem of his style, which must be studied in terms of alienation and reification" (159), for "*style* in Dreiser [is] a strange and alien bodily speech . . . interwoven with the linguistic junk of commodified language" (160-1). Accordingly, "the tawdriness of Carrie's hunger for trinkets [is] a tawdriness that Dreiser's language ambiguously represents and reflects all at once" (159). Sandy Petrey finds similar examples of commodification and "false consciousness" in Dreiser's use of melodramatic and sentimental language, which Petrey links to capitalist mass-media forms, such as popular songs. Walter Benn Michaels also argues for a complex and comprehensive connection between economics and fictional narrative, proposing that Dreiser's strategies of novelistic representation suggest an important affinity between naturalism and capitalism insofar as naturalist fiction and consumer capitalism are structured and sustained by similar formulations of personal identity and desire, whereby "satisfaction itself is never desirable" (42). For these and other critics, the point is not just that economics constitutes the subject matter of *Sister Carrie*, but more importantly that narrative form and technique are themselves modes of production linked to economic conditions and concepts.

These economic interpretations all address the considerable attention Dreiser gives to desire, which provides a sort of organizational map for tracking and differentiating a number of novelistic and economic configurations. Walter Benn Michaels, for example, argues that "Carrie; for Dreiser, embodies insatiability" (56), whereas Hurstwood ultimately signifies "exhausted desire and economic failure" (46), thereby suggesting that characters' economic positions can be organized along a bipolar axis of desire and indifference. Michaels places Carrie's desire "inside" the logic of consumption, whereas Hurstwood's indifference in the end locates him "outside" the "walled city" of this narrative economy of desire. Hurstwood dies an indifferent death because he wants nothing, whereas Carrie goes on by a "principle of discrepancy" in which her identity is articulated and sustained in the difference between what she is and what she wants. While other critics have challenged Michaels' narrow emphasis on desire, they nevertheless replicate a similar binary formula of individual desire and naturalistic indifference in which the latter variously signifies the resistance to, or absence of, desire. Moreover, Dreiser's naturalist theater of indifference tends to lead critics to argue that Hurstwood's position is somehow more authentic or real or honest than Carrie's. This distinction, in turn, is but one link in a whole chain of related oppositions, in which Carrie and Hurstwood, desire and satisfaction, illusion and reality, economic consumption and production, and even the stylistic mix of Dreiser's "commodified language" and naturalist verity can all be aligned into an impressive, albeit problematically ambivalent, critique of consumer capitalism.[2]

What does not get much attention in these critical interpretations is the role of indifference in such formulations, except for rather casual references to conventional descriptions of naturalism's propensity for rendering its characters in a universe of deterministic mechanism, impersonal force, and entropic decline. Indifference here functions as a sort of master-signifier of all that which opposes individual desire or marks its absence. To some extent, this equation is useful, but it tends to result in an overdetermined representation of desire and indifference as distinct and stable oppositional identities, whereas they are more like two aspects of a single structural process. (Indeed, "indifference" is a rather evocative word for deconstructionist play.) Throughout *Sister Carrie*, characters are variously identified and related to each other as subjects and objects of desire and indifference, which structure and sustain each other in a series of exchanges both real and imagined. Configurations of desire and indifference operate at the level of both personal drama and social narrative, and therefore significantly inform the entire fictional economy of *Sister Carrie.*

For example, Carrie's early desire to find a job takes her along a path whose contours are significantly mapped by indifference. In her first venture into the streets of Chicago, she is

> conscious of being gazed upon and understood for what she was—a wage-seeker. . . . To avoid a certain indefinable shame she felt at being caught spying for a position, she quickened her steps and assumed an air of indifference supposedly common to one upon an errand. (18)

Once inside the department stores, Carrie, who is "not familiar with the appearance of her more fortunate sisters in the city," notices that they are "pretty in the main, some even handsome, with an air of independence and indifference, which added, in the case of the more favoured, a certain piquancy" (23). Toward the end of a long first day of job-hunting, Carrie's "fatigued senses" instill in her the notion that "the great business portion grew larger, harder, more stolid in its indifference. It seemed as if it was all closed to her" (26).

A second episode suggests a similar configuration of desire and indifference in a market of a different sort. Some time after she is established as Drouet's mistress, Carrie goes to the theater with Drouet and Hurstwood. At the theater we watch a performance of what Dreiser refers to as "the ancient attraction of the fresh for the stale" (92). This show, however, is not on the stage, but in the box in which Carrie's desire for Drouet diminishes as her attraction to Hurstwood rises. Carrie is "pleased beyond expression" with Hurstwood: "Several times their eyes accidentally met, and then there poured into hers such a flood of feeling as she had never before experienced. She could not for the moment explain it, for in the next glance or the next move of the hand there was seeming indifference, mingled only with the kindest attention." Later, he takes Carrie's "little hand" to wish her goodnight, and a "current of feeling" sweeps from one to the other (96-7).

In these two episodes, indifference is alternately a source of desire (that which makes you piquant), a mask for desire (that which hides your hunger), and a path along which desire arrives at satisfaction. Critics have themselves remained indifferent to Dreiser's rather habitual use of the word "indifference," although it appears in *Sister Carrie* so often that the attending reader might feel compelled to ask whether it is only another of Dreiser's often-noted stylistic blemishes, an example of how

Dreiser rather heavy-handedly inscribes a major theme into the novel by literally and repeatedly smuggling its name into the text, or a usage of more provocative significance. Perhaps Dreiser's use of "indifference" is a kind of "fault" in the text in the sense of both "defect or error" and "break or rupture," or, alternately, an "oversight" that marks both careless mistake and watchful management. Given the considerable critical analysis of desire in *Sister Carrie*, this closely related motif in Dreiser's work deserves more attention.

II. NEOCLASSICAL DESIRE AND INDIFFERENCE

Neoclassical economic analysis, especially its marginal utility theory of consumer behavior, offers a useful model for exploring desire and indifference in *Sister Carrie*. While the novel has indeed attracted many economic readings of desire, critics have tended toward Marxist interpretations or other approaches outside the mainstream neoclassical tradition, such as Thorstein Veblen's "institutionalist" analysis of consumer capitalism.[3] Generally, literary critics have been indifferent to neoclassical economic theory in their readings of *Sister Carrie*, although the emergence of that discourse is historically coincident with Dreiser's novel. Moreover, like *Sister Carrie*, neoclassical analysis addresses the connections between the subjective desire of the individual consumer and objective market conditions. Between the 1870s and the early years of the twentieth century, the work of neoclassical economists such as W. S. Jevons and Alfred Marshall in England, Carl Menger in Austria, Leon Walras and Vilfredo Pareto in Switzerland, and John Bates Clark in the United States marks a significant change in mainstream economic analysis. Although they were largely unaware of each other's efforts, their work suggests a kind of harmonic convergence that, depending on one's interpretive apparatus, variously looks like disciplinary breakthrough, capitalist conspiracy, or Foucauldian episteme.[4]

One important feature of the neoclassical project is that whereas classical economists generally sought to explain market prices by a theory of value based on production costs, neoclassical economists shifted their attention to individual consumption utility. Moreover, they addressed economic utility by way of "rates of exchange," in which, to put it in terms of Saussure's suggestively and historically coincidental formulation, "there are only differences, *without positive terms*." For example, Carrie's shoes would have no inherent value based solely on the objective costs of their production (such as the labor "embodied" in them). Instead, they provide Carrie with a particular level of utility that she would assign to them according to their relative usefulness and scarcity in a system of commodities. Carrie's utility assignments are both subjective and contingent, but are nevertheless empirically revealed in her manifest consumer choices.

Neoclassical marginal utility theory argues that, while we cannot know utility in any absolute sense, we can *compare* the utility of different objects of desire in relation to one another in terms of revealed preferences and exchanges. Anticipating Dreiser's naturalistic formulation of desire, Jevons claimed in 1871 that his goal was to "treat Economy as a Calculus of Pleasure and Pain" (vi) in which a "mechanics of utility and self-interest" (21) could be rigorously constructed. Although "every mind is . . . inscrutable to every other mind, and no common denominator seems to be possible" (14) Jevons insisted that "the Laws of Exchange . . . resemble the Laws of Equilibrium of a Lever" (vii). Similarly, Pareto argued that the "theory of economic science thus acquires the rigor of rational mechanics; it deduces its results from experience, without bringing in any metaphysical entity" (113).

Neoclassical economists such as Jevons and Pareto attempted to do away with absolute values altogether by using the concept of indifference to signify desire in a system of relative differences. As Jevons put it, "if we can compare the quantities . . . we do not need the units" (12). In their analyses, indifference refers to a particular set of consumer choices in which each choice represents the same total utility. An indifference curve might depict the range of consumption trade-offs between shoes and jackets that give Carrie a certain level of pleasure, hence she is indifferent between any two positions on that schedule. The "shape" of his schedule or curve is determined by the rate at which she would be willing to exchange shoes for jackets, which is a function of their relative usefulness and scarcity as Carrie perceives them. An indifference map consists of a number of indifference curves (something like a topographical map), each of which depicts a certain level of utility. From this indifference map we can determine where Carrie maximizes her utility, given the constraints of prices and income.

Perhaps this short description is both too much and not enough for economists and non-economists alike, but the main point to keep in mind is that the neoclassical model argues that because individual desire is subjective and objective conditions are variable, economic utility has meaning only in a system of relative differences. Moreover, utility is maximized where these different desires are somehow in (equimarginal) balance, by way of what Jevons called the "law of indifference." Note that in the neoclassical model, indifference does not delineate a static or entropic state of equilibrium in which individual desire is absent, exhausted, or resisted, nor does indifference signify those material conditions of "the real" that impinge upon desire, such as the alienating effects of the capitalist market system. Instead, desire is, as it were, alive and well.

Sister Carrie resonates with much of this, although it would be difficult to argue that Carrie or any other character functions strictly like a mimetic representation of the neoclassical utility maximizer. This would be no more satisfactory than overdetermined Marxist readings. Yet the neoclassical model does provide a suggestive trope for the fictional economy of *Sister Carrie*. First, personal desire and satisfaction, as well as the social causes and consequences of those personal states, are significantly rendered in terms of economic consumption—perhaps as much as anything, Carrie is a consumer. Second, the utilities of those objects that characters desire are subjective and variable. We note, for example, that Carrie moves through a landscape significantly mapped in terms of differences, an array of commodities, people, and social positions whose identities she knows and values in terms of their relative positions. Just as her ideas about clothing styles, furnishings, and restaurants keep evolving as one observation and experience replaces another, so too does she tend to assign value to Drouet, Hurstwood, and Ames in relation to one another. Third, Carrie repeatedly makes these trade-offs in terms of the conventional economic utility function, in which the "diminishing returns" of various objects, people, places, and predicaments delineate her narrative path. This is what is referred to early in the novel as "the ancient attraction of the fresh for the stale" (92). Fourth, Carrie engages in some utilitarian cost-benefit analysis of her decisions, such as when she weighs the ethical costs against the economic gains of her association with Drouet, or in shopping sprees in which she is in the "delightful . . . middle state in which we mentally balance at times, possessed of the means, lured by desire, and yet deterred by conscience or want of decision" (61). Moreover, Dreiser makes these predicaments interpersonal in ways that resemble Jevons' notion of the "laws of equilibrium of a lever":

> "Oh," thought Drouet, "how delicious is my conquest."
>
> "Ah," thought Carrie, with mournful misgivings, "what is it I have lost?" (81)

In all of these aspects we note how the novel, like neoclassical utility theory, combines subjective states and objective outcomes in a way that should caution against reductive applications of a strictly deterministic and mechanistic philosophy. Arguing for a link between Dreiserian naturalism and the neoclassical model of individual agency is therefore really not so surprising when one considers the extent to which, in spite of Dreiser's expository riffs about "the forces which sweep and play throughout the universe" (67), much of the fiction is organized around isolated individuals, their subjective states, and their conscious deliberations. Conversely, neoclassical utility theory, with its formally mechanistic configurations of force and equilibrium, also resonates with those traditionally cited aspects of naturalism.

III. INDIFFERENCE AND THE CONDUCT OF DESIRE

Indifference is cast too variously by Dreiser to be read only as a figuration of naturalistic force. Instead, throughout the novel indifference is both personal and impersonal, desired and dreaded, and imagined as real and represented as artificial. Indifference organizes characters as both subjects and objects, functions dramatically within scenes, and organizes structural and dynamic exchanges between them. A more extensive survey of indifference in the novel amplifies these key points.

Carrie's introduction to Chicago begins with her sense that for her brother-in-law Hanson, she is "a matter of indifference" (13), which isolates Carrie and compels her movement away from the household. So, while indifference has an alienating effect on Carrie, this alienation is nevertheless a kind of dramatic engine that drives her out of the domestic sphere and into the economic marketplace. On the other hand, indifference is neither solely personal nor entirely "real," as is suggested in the examples of her initial job search and trip to the theater with Hurstwood. Similarly, in one of his earliest and most effective declarations of affection for Carrie, Hurstwood says to her,

> "You think . . . I am happy . . . ? If you were to meet all day with people who care absolutely nothing about you, if you went day after day to a place where there was nothing but show and indifference, if there was not one person . . . to whom you could appeal for sympathy or talk to with pleasure, perhaps you would be unhappy too." (111)

In this instance, Hurstwood's reference to indifference, like Dreiser's usage more generally, is ambiguous in at least three ways. First, it is not clear here whether indifference is a kind of performance in apposition to "show," or is instead some "real" condition that delineates the production of such an illusion. Second, the business of indifference, which Hurstwood claims is grinding him down, is nevertheless a condition of his success as a manager of a public establishment insofar as he has to maintain a certain social persona. Finally, his depiction of the "public" indifference does "personal" work in the scene, for it functions as an attractor between him and Carrie.

This attraction between Hurstwood and Carrie parallels the growing "river of indifference" (120) between Hurstwood and his wife, as well as within the Hurstwood household more generally. When Mrs. Hurstwood insists upon being given the "Waukesha money," she "turned upon [Hurstwood], animal-like, able to strike" and he looks at her "in amazement. Never before had he seen such a cold, steely determination in her eye—such a look of indifference" (182). Here again Dreiser either strains the usage of the word (conflating determination and indifference) or implies that the indifference is merely a mask—a kind of theatrical show intended to have a desired effect. Similarly, Carrie's encounters with other women in her first job search is replicated in the description of Hurstwood's daughter Jessica, who is characterized by her "cynical indifference," and whose "independence and indifference" is studiously asserted "with a toss of her head and a flick of her pretty skirts" (175).

These examples suggest how configurations of indifference and desire not only operate *within* scenes, but also organize the relationship *between* them, especially in terms of the patterns of repetition and transformation in the forward-moving narrative. For example, when Carrie leaves Drouet and retraces her steps in order to look for work again, she notices a difference:

> She knew that she had improved in appearance. . . . men . . . who before had gazed at her indifferently from behind their polished railings and imposing office partitions—now gazed into her face with a soft light in their eyes. . . . she felt the power and satisfaction of the thing. (206)

In this instance, Carrie conveys rather than encounters indifference, marking a shift in power; she is, as it were, a producer rather than a consumer of indifference. The economy of desire and indifference within the earlier episode is replicated in a narrative structure by which the *différance* of indifference, we might say, narrates Carrie's progress. Similarly, when Carrie later ventures out into the theater world of New York, indifference shapes the exchange much as it does her first job search: "At the Empire Theatre she found a hive of peculiarly listless and indifferent individuals" (316) and in an interview she "tried to be calm and indifferent, but it was a palpable sham" (318). Once she becomes a successful star, however, she "smiled to think that men should suddenly find her so much more attractive. In the least way it incited her to coolness and indifference" (379).

Likewise, in her attraction to Ames, Carrie replicates her earlier attraction to Drouet and Hurstwood, in which indifference circulates as cause and effect of desire, both of which are ambiguously real and artificial. Carrie finds that Ames "reminded her of scenes she had seen on the stage" and that he "had taken away some of the bitterness of the contrast between this life and her life, and all by a certain calm indifference which concerned only him." This is, she thinks, quite different from the "feigned indifference" she projects at their parting (272). She later attempts to "get" some of this "better" indifference by reading the naturalist novel that Ames has recommended to her (Balzac's *Pere Goriot*).

Even so, there is no getting "outside" Dreiser's fictional economy of the production and consumption of indifference, for in the last "real" scene with Carrie, she is in her "comfortable chambers at the Waldorf . . . reading at this time 'Pere Goriot' " (411). Shamed by her earlier readings as "silly and worthless" fictional representations, she "nearly caught the full sympathetic significance" of Balzac's naturalist story. "Becoming wearied, however, she yawned and came to the window, looking out upon the old winding procession of carriages rolling up Fifth Avenue" (411). Carrie substitutes the spectacle of the window for the naturalist picture in Balzac's novel, yet both result in a similar indifference. As they watch the storm outside, Carrie chides her friend Lola for her indifference toward those who have nothing, yet Carrie is herself indifferent to Lola's observation at the sight of some "sheepish" man falling in the snow, for Carrie is thinking "absently" now of their need for a coach. At the end, Carrie finds that what were "once far off, essential things" such as money, fame, and beauty have "grown trivial and indifferent" (416), Dreiser's final, awkward use of the word that entirely conflates subjects and objects in a matrix of indifference. Like Carrie's famous theatrical pout, Dreiserian indifference carries much of the show.

In *Sister Carrie*, then, people are always looking or being looked at in an exchange that always involves some blend of desire and indifference. The novel begins with Carrie boarding the afternoon train for Chicago, and she is from the start both spectacle ("her total outfit consisted of a small trunk, a cheap imitation alligator-skin satchel, a small lunch in a paper box, and a yellow leather snap purse") and spectator:

> A gush of tears . . . a touch in her throat when the cars clacked by the flour mill . . . a pathetic sigh as the familiar green environs of the village passed in review . . . . She gazed at the green landscape now passing in swift review, until her swifter thoughts replaced its impression with vague conjectures. (5)

We look at Carrie looking at her imaginary representations of Chicago, which are "swifter thoughts" that substitute for the reality of the passing "green landscape," which has itself already become a kind of imagined pastoral recollection in Dreiser's fiction.

And in spite of Carrie's attraction for the lamp-lit "promise of night" (11), we ought not forget the way in which the daytime reality of economic production also puts itself on display for visual consumption:

> The large plates of window glass, now so common, were then rapidly coming into use, and gave to the ground floor offices a distinguished and prosperous look. The casual wanderer could see as he passed a polished array of office fixtures, much frosted glass, clerks hard at work, and genteel business men in 'nobby' suits and clean linen lounging about or sitting in groups. . . . The entire metropolitan centre possessed a high and mighty air calculated to overawe and abash the common applicant, and to make the gulf between poverty and success seem both wide and deep. (17)

Here the medium of glass is simultaneously transparent and reflective, a configuration in which desire is produced (in Carrie) in a show of indifference (by the world of commerce). Later, when she gets her first job, Carrie thinks, "Ah, the long winter in Chicago—the lights, the crowd, and amusement! This was a great, pleasing metropolis after all. Her new firm was a goodly institution. Its windows were of huge plate glass" (28). She exclaims to her sister and brother-in-law, "'It seems to be such a large company . . . . Great big plate-glass windows and lots of clerks" (28).

It is not quite accurate, therefore, to say that Carrie moves increasingly from sites of production to consumption, for she is from the beginning already there. Production is "always already" coded as consumption in terms of its configuration as visual display. Dreiser's naturalist observation of material conditions is closely tied to Carrie's own enthrallment with the displays of the plate glass windows of business, the glass counters in department stores, and her own image in the glass mirror. From the beginning, Carrie's predicament is linked to this representation of consumer display. Even on the train to Chicago in the opening scene, when Drouet makes mention of the clothier and dry goods shops in her home town, she is "aroused by memories of longings their show windows had cost her" (8). Again we see how in *Sister Carrie,* we can imagine some pre-consumer reality only as pastoral nostalgia in a naturalist shop window.

Like artificial lights and transparent glass, mirrors are an important conductor of desire and indifference. An early example of this occurs when Drouet and Carrie go shopping for clothes. When Carrie tries on the first jacket, Dreiser uses subtle switches in point of view and light imagery to duplicate the reflective exchange suggested by the mirror. Also, remember that even the jacket is a kind of simulacrum which is more "real" than the "original" at The Fair:

> Together they went. In the store they found that shine and rustle of new things which immediately laid hold of Carrie's heart. . . . She looked about and picked up a jacket like the one she had admired at The Fair. When she got it in her hand it seemed so much nicer. The saleswoman helped her on with it, and, by accident, it fitted perfectly. Drouet's face lightened as he saw the improvement. She looked quite smart.
>
> "That's the thing," he said.
>
> Carrie turned before the glass. She could not help feeling pleased as she looked at herself. A warm glow crept into her cheeks.
>
> "That's the thing," said Drouet. "Now pay for it." (64)

The same exchange repeats itself as they buy shoes, a purse, gloves, and stockings. As Carrie becomes more involved with Drouet, a pattern of reflection and desire emerges:

> at last she looked like quite another maiden. The mirror convinced her of a few things which she had long believed. She was pretty, yes indeed! How nice her hat set, and weren't her eyes pretty. She caught her little red lip with her teeth and felt her first thrill of power. (69)

Furthermore, Carrie's vacillations involving ethical and aesthetic reflection resist any clear and stable distinction between real and reflected identity: "She looked into her glass and saw a prettier Carrie than she had seen before; she looked into her mind, a mirror prepared of her own and the world's opinions, and saw a worse. Between these two images she wavered, hesitating which to believe." The conflict, then, is not between some notion of the "authentic" Carrie in danger of losing her "real" self, for what she is losing is but another reflection: "It was only an average little conscience, a thing which represented the world, her environment, habit, convention, in a confused way" (82).

Throughout the novel Dreiser uses images of light, glass, and mirrors to situate subjects and objects in a representational field of desire and indifference that goes beyond characters' self-representation and relations with each other to include the narrator and reader as well. For example, when we learn of Drouet's fondness for Fitzgerald's and Moy's, the attraction is described in terms of the

> blaze of incandescent lights . . . handsome chandeliers. . . . brightly colored tiles . . . polished wood, which reflected the light . . . . The long bar was a blaze of lights . . . coloured and cut glassware, and many fancy bottles. It was truly a swell saloon. (40)

Here Dreiser depicts an object of desire informed by light, glass, and reflective imagery, all of which are looked at by one desiring subject—Drouet—and an indifferent other—Hurstwood, who stands "outside" this field:

> To one not inclined to drink, and gifted with a more serious turn of mind, such a bubbling, chattering, glittering chamber must ever seem an anomaly . . . . Here come the moths, in endless procession, to bask in the light of the flame. . . . the fact . . . must be explained upon some grounds. It must be that a strange bundle of passions and vague desires give rise to such a curious social institution or it would not be. (43)

In this scene, then, we have a juxtapositioning of both desiring and indifferent subjects—not only Drouet and Hurstwood, but also the hypothetical viewer who is not quite out in the cold:

> here is the fact of the lighted chamber . . . the love of light and show and finery which, to one outside, under the serene light of the eternal stars, must seem a strange and shiny thing. Under the stars and sweeping night winds, what a lamp-flower it must bloom; a strange, glittering night-flower, odour-yielding, insect-drawing, insect-infected rose of pleasure. (44)

This dynamic is also operative in terms of Dreiser's broader plot structure. When Drouet and Carrie go to eat at the Windsor, Drouet selects a table "close by the window, where the busy route of the street could be seen. He loved the changing panorama of the street—to see and be seen as he dined" (53). This imagined set of specular seating assignments is replicated when Carrie goes to Sherry's with the Vances and Ames (Hurstwood, indifferent, stays home). Here the sense of being "inside" is constituted in part by an "outside" position. Again, the imagery of light and glass suggest the tropes of looking and reflection:

> In all Carrie's experience she had never seen anything like this. . . . Carrie had read of it often . . . . She had seen notices . . . . [which] had given her a distinct idea of the gorgeousness and luxury of this wonderful temple . . . . Now, at last, she was really in it. . . . Here was the splendid dining-chamber, all decorated and aglow . . . . Vance led the way through lanes of shining tables . . . . Incandescent lights, the reflection of their glow in polished glasses, and the shine of gilt upon the walls, combined into one tone of light which it requires minutes of complacent observation to separate and take note of. (267-8)

Later, Hurstwood occupies the position of outsider looking in with a very different sort of "complacent observation." When he is on his last walk through the city, starving, cold, and suicidal,

> he paused in an aimless, incoherent way and looked through the windows of an imposing restaurant, before which blazed a fire sign, and through the large, plate windows of which could be seen the red and gold decorations, the palms, the white napery, and shining glassware, and above all, the comfortable crowd. Weak as his mind had become, his hunger was sharp enough to show the importance of this. He stopped stock still, his frayed trousers soaking in the slush, and peered foolishly in.
>
> "Eat," he mumbled. "That's right, eat. Nobody else wants any." (410)

Desire and indifference circulate inside and outside of restaurants to constitute characters' sense of predicament and identity *and* Dreiser's strategy for representing those conditions. Hurstwood's position of indifference completes the stagecraft of desire:

> At Broadway and Thirty-ninth Street was a blazing, in incandescent fire, Carrie's name. 'Carrie Madenda,' it read . . . . All the wet, snowy sidewalk was bright with this radiated fire. It was so bright that it attracted Hurstwood's gaze. He looked up, and then at a large, gilt-framed poster-board, on which was a fine lithograph of Carrie, life-size.

> Hurstwood gazed at it a moment, snuffling and hunching one shoulder, as if something were scratching him. He was so run down, however, that his mind was not exactly clear.
>
> "That's you," he said at last, addressing her. (410)

Hungry, penniless, mentally deranged, emptied out of all desire, Hurstwood's indifference is nevertheless very much a working part of this naturalist economy of desire. In this way, Carrie's desire to be the "cynosure of all eyes" and "compel acknowledgement of power" (135) is structured and sustained by Dreiser's broader novelistic deployment of indifference.

IV. A COINCIDENCE AND A QUERY

Although neoclassical economic theory might be judged by many literary critics (and economists) as an unsatisfactory representation of behavior because of its mechanistic model of conscious, rational, and unified subjects maximizing utility, it also presents something like those post-structuralist notions of identity, difference, and desire that contemporary critics often deploy to read *Sister Carrie*. Indeed, anyone familiar with Ferdinand de Saussure's structuralist linguistics (or its impact on literary criticism) will recognize something like familiar territory in neoclassical economics. In *Course in General Linguistics* Saussure points to his neoclassical contemporaries as an example to be emulated by linguists:

> Very few linguists suspect that the intervention of the factor of time creates difficulties peculiar to linguistics and opens to their science two completely different paths. . . . Most other sciences are unaffected by this radical duality . . . . On the contrary, that duality is already forcing itself upon the economic sciences. Here, in contrast to the other sciences, political economy and economic history constitute two clearly separated disciplines within a single science; the works that have recently appeared on these subjects point up the distinction. Proceeding as they have, economists are—without being well aware of it—obeying an inner necessity. A similar necessity obliges us to divide linguistics into two parts, each with its own principle. Here as in political economy we are confronted with the notion of *value*; both sciences are concerned with *a system for equating things of different orders* . . . . (79)

However, while Saussure makes a strong connection between linguistics and economics, he nevertheless insists on a difference:

> language is a system of pure values which are determined by nothing except the momentary arrangement of its terms. A value—so long as it is somehow rooted in things and in their natural relations, as happens with economics . . . can to some extent be traced in time if we remember that it depends at each moment upon a system of coexisting values. Its link with things gives it, perforce, a natural basis, and the judgments that we base on such values are therefore never completely arbitrary; their variability is limited. But we have just seen that natural data have no place in linguistics. (80)

But neoclassical formalism generally and its approach to utility specifically does point to the affinities with structuralist linguistics. One interesting historical caveat is the evidence of contact and exchange between Saussure and the neoclassical economists Walras and Pareto, as is suggested in Julien Freund's claim that Pareto maintained "excellent relations" with Saussure and that Pareto's references to connections between linguistics and sociology can be partly explained in terms of his friendship with Saussure (27-8).

My purpose here is not to establish a determined paper trail of influence between economics and linguistics (and therefore critical theory). I do hope, however, that this reading of *Sister Carrie* would suggest that the widespread lack of interest of literary critics in this area of economic thought ought to be addressed by more work in a number of interdisciplinary directions involving connections between neoclassical economics and literary study. The absence of neoclassical theory in economic readings of *Sister Carrie* is especially problematic, given the historical correspondence between neoclassical economics and naturalism, the similarities between neoclassical analysis and the economic issues that critics observe in the novel, and the curious coincidence between neoclassical economics and contemporary poststructuralist reading strategies. However we might want to speculate on such critical desire and indifference, the "coincidence of wants" between neoclassical economics, *Sister Carrie*, and its critical reception speaks to Fredric Jameson's Marxist insistence to "always historicize," for there has occurred a kind of critical forgetting which is in need of being remembered and remedied.

NOTES

[1] Most readings of *Sister Carrie* at least note this configuration. The novelistic structure is typically linked to Herbert Spencer's concepts of equilibrium, which is said to have influenced Dreiser's naturalistic representation of economic

conditions. For more extensive analysis of Spencer's influence on Dreiser, see Martin, Katope, and Zanine.

[2] For other examples of this pattern, see Lehan, See, and Shulman. For an interesting exception to this pattern, see Kaplan, who writes, "In *Sister Carrie* . . . Dreiser achieves something like the [mimetic] transparency for which Howells and Norris longed, and he is able to do so, apparently, because he ignores Howells' and Norris's assumptions about the location of the 'real,' about the distinction between 'reality' and 'style'" (165).

[3] Michaels, Jameson, and Petrey all use Marxist theory extensively. For a good example of an economic reading making use of Veblen, see Eby.

[4] As many historians of economic thought point out, this attention to utility and value was by no means without precedent. Mentioning other Continental economists such as Quesney, Beccaria, Turgot, and Bernoulli, Joseph Schumpeter argues that this strain of analysis "had wind until the influence of [Adam Smith's] *Wealth of Nations*—and especially Ricardo's *Principles*—asserted itself" (300-2). Also, for related discussions of the psychology of desire, modern subjectivity, and economic utility, see Foucault 166-216 and Goux.

Bibliography

Armstrong, Nancy. *Desire and Domestic Fiction: A Political History of the Novel*. New York: Oxford UP, 1987.

Bahktin, M. M. *The Dialogic Imagination*. Ed. Michael Holquist. Trans. Caryl Emerson and Michael Holquist. Austin: U of Texas P, 1981.

Bell, Ian A. "Narrators and Narrative in Defoe." *Novel: A Forum on Fiction* 18.2 (1985): 154-172.

Blaug, Mark. *Economic Theory in Retrospect*. 4th ed. Cambridge: Cambridge UP, 1985.

Böhm-Bawerk, Eugen V. *The Positive Theory of Capital*. London: Macmillan, 1891.

Bowlby, Rachel. *Just Looking: Consumer Culture in Dreiser, Gissing, and Zola*. New York: Methuen, 1985.

Braverman, Richard. "Crusoe's Legacy." *Studies in the Novel* 18.1 (1986): 1-26.

Brennan, Stephen C. "The Two Endings of *Sister Carrie*." *Studies in American Fiction* 16.1 (1988): 13-26.

Brooks, Peter. *Reading for the Plot*. New York: Knopf, 1984.

Brown, Gillian. "The Empire of Agoraphobia." *Representations* 20 (1987): 134-157.

Brown, Homer O. "The Displaced Self in the Novels of Daniel Defoe." *English Literary History* 38.4 (1971): 562-90.

Butler, Mary E. "The Effect of the Narrator's Rhetorical Uncertainty on the Fiction of *Robinson Crusoe*." *Studies in the Novel* 25.2 (1983): 77-90.

Cantillon, Richard. *Essai sur la nature de la commerce en général*. Ed. H. Higgs. London: Macmillan, 1931.

Cipolla, Carlo M. *Money, Prices, and Civilization in the Mediterranean World: Fifth to Seventeenth Century*. Cincinnati: U of Cincinnati P, 1956.

Coetzee, J. M. *Foe*. New York: Penguin, 1986.

Davidson, Cathy N. *Revolution and the Word: The Rise of the Novel in America*. New York: Oxford UP, 1986.

Defoe, Daniel. *Robinson Crusoe*. Ed. Michael Shinagel. New York: W. W. Norton, 1975.

Dreiser, Theodore. *Sister Carrie*. Ed. Claude Simpson. Boston: Houghton Mifflin, 1959.

Eby, Clare Virginia. *Dreiser and Veblen, Saboteurs of the Status Quo*. Columbia: U of Missouri P, 1998.

Ekelund, Robert B. Jr. and Robert F. Hebert. *A History of Economic Theory and Method*. New York: McGraw-Hill, 1990.

Ellis, Kate. "Monsters in the Garden: Mary Shelley and the Bourgeois Family." Levine and Knoepflmacher, 123-142.

Erickson, Robert A. "Starting Over with *Robinson Crusoe*." *Studies in the Literary Imagination* 15.2 (1982): 51-73.

Foucault, Michel. *The Order of Things: An Archeology of the Human Sciences*. New York: Vintage, 1973.

Freud, Sigmund. *Beyond the Pleasure Principle*. Trans. and Ed. James Strachey. New York: W. W. Norton, 1961.

Freund, Julien. *Pareto*. Trans. Simona Draghica. Washington: Plutarch Press, 1986.

Goldmann, Lucien. *Towards a Sociology of the Novel*. Trans. Alan Sheridan. London: Tavistock, 1975.

Goux, Jean Joseph. "The Calculation of Jouissance." *Symbolic Economies: After Marx and Freud*. Trans. Jennifer Curtiss Gage. Ithaca: Cornell UP, 1990.

Heinzelman, Kurt. *The Economics of the Imagination*. Amherst: U of Massachusetts P, 1980.

Henry, John F. *The Making of Neoclassical Economics*. Boston: Unwin Hyman, 1990.

Hulme, Peter. *Colonial Encounters: Europe and the Native Caribbean, 1492-1797*. New York: Metheun, 1986.

Hume, David. *Essays Moral, Political, and Literary*. Ed. T. H. Green and T. H. Grose. London: Longmans, Green & Co., 1907.

Hunter, Paul J. *The Reluctant Pilgrim: Defoe's Emblematic Method and Quest for Form in Robinson Crusoe*. Baltimore: Johns Hopkins UP, 1966.

Hussman, Lawrence E., Jr., *Dreiser and His Fiction: A Twentieth-Century Quest*. Philadelphia: U of Pennsylvania P, 1983.

Hymer, Stephen. "*Robinson Crusoe* and the Secret of Primitive Accumulation." *Monthly Review* 23.4 (1971): 11-36.

Jameson, Fredric. *The Political Unconscious: Narrative as a Socially Symbolic Act*. Ithaca: Cornell UP, 1981.

Jevons, William Stanley. *The Theory of Political Economy*. 5th ed. New York: Sentry, 1965.

Kaplan, Amy. *The Social Construction of American Realism*. Chicago: U of Chicago P, 1988.

Katope, Christopher G. "*Sister Carrie* and Spencer's *First Principles*." *American Literature* 41 (1969): 64-75.

Kaufmann, David. *The Business of Common Life: Novels and Classical Economics between Revolution and Reform*. Baltimore: Johns Hopkins UP, 1994.

Klamer, Arlo, Donald A. McCloskey, and Robert M. Solow, eds. *The Consequences of Economic Rhetoric*. Cambridge: Cambridge UP, 1988.

Lehan, Richard. "*Sister Carrie*: The City, the Self, and the Modes of Narrative Discourse." Pizer, *New Essays*, 65-85.

Levine, George and U. C. Knoepfmacher, eds. *The Endurance of Frankenstein: Essays on Mary Shelley's Novel*. Berkeley: U of California P, 1979.

Lukács, George. *Theory of the Novel*. Trans. Anna Bostock. Cambridge: M.I.T. Press, 1971.

Male, Roy R., ed. *Money Talks: Language and Lucre in American Fiction*. Norman: U of Oklahoma P, 1980.

Marshall, Alfred. *Principles of Economics*. 8th ed. London: Macmillan, 1930.

Martin, Ronald E. *American Literature and the Universe of Force*. Durham: Duke UP, 1993.

Mathiessen, F. O. "A Picture of Conditions." *Theodore Dreiser*. New York: Sloan, 1951. 59-88.

McCloskey, Donald N. *If You're So Smart: The Narrative of Economic Expertise*. Chicago: U of Chicago P, 1990.

———. *The Rhetoric of Economics*. Madison: U of Wisconsin P, 1985.

McKeon, Michael. *The Origins of the English Novel, 1600-1744*. Baltimore: The Johns Hopkins UP, 1987.

Melville, Herman. *Moby Dick*. Ed. Alfred Kazin. Boston: Houghton Mifflin-Riverside Editions, 1956.

Michaels, Walter Benn. *The Gold Standard and the Logic of Naturalism*. Berkeley: U California P, 1987.

Michie, Elsie. "*Frankenstein* and Marx's Theories of Alienated Labor." *Approaches to Teaching Shelley's Frankenstein*. Ed. Stephen C. Behrendt. New York: Modern Language Association of America, 1990. 93-8.

Mill, John Stuart. *Principles of Political Economy*. Ed. W. J. Ashley. New York: A. M. Kelley, 1965.

Mirowski, Philip. *More Heat than Light: Economics as Social Physics: Physics as Nature's Economics*. Cambridge: Cambridge UP, 1989.

Montag, Warren. "'The Workshop of Filthy Creation': A Marxist Reading of *Frankenstein*." *Frankenstein: Case Studies in Contemporary Criticism*. Ed. Johanna M. Smith. Boston: St. Martin's Press, 1992. 300-11.

Moretti, Franco. *Signs Taken for Wonders: Essays in the Sociology of Literary Forms*. Trans. Susan Fisher, David Forgacs, and David Miller. London: Verso, 1983.

Novak, Maximillian E. *Economics and the Fiction of Daniel Defoe*. Berkeley: U of California P, 1962.

Olson, Charles. *Call Me Ishmael*. San Francisco: City Lights, 1947.

Pareto, Vilfredo. *Manual of Political Economy*. Trans. Ann S. Schwier. Ed. Schwier and Alfred N. Page. New York: Augustus M. Kelley Publishers, 1971.

Petrey, Sandy. "The Language of Realism, The Language of False Consciousness: A Reading of *Sister Carrie*." *Novel: A Forum on Fiction* 10 (1977): 101-13.

Pizer, Donald, ed. *Critical Essays on Theodore Dreiser*. Boston: G. K. Hall, 1981.

———. *New Essays on Sister Carrie*. Cambridge: Cambridge UP, 1991.

———. *The Novels of Theodore Dreiser: A Critical Study*. Minneapolis: U of Minnesota P, 1976.

———. *The Theory and Practice of American Literary Naturalism*. Carbondale: Southern Illinois UP, 1993.

Ramsey, Peter H., ed. *The Price Revolution in Sixteenth Century England*. London: Methuen, 1971.

Richetti, John J. *Daniel Defoe*. Boston: G.K. Hall, 1987.

Rogin, Paul. *Subversive Genealogy: The Politics and Art of Herman Melville*. New York: Knopf, 1983..

Said, Edward W. *Beginnings: Intention and Method*. New York: Columbia UP, 1975.

———. *Culture and Imperialism*. New York: Knopf, 1993.

———. *Orientalism*. New York: Pantheon, 1978.

Saussure, Ferdinand de. *Course in General Linguistics*. Trans. Wade Baskin. Bungay, Suffolk England: Fontana/Collins, 1974.

See, Fred G. "The Text as Mirror: 'Sister Carrie' and the Lost Language of the Heart." *Criticism: A Quarterly for Literature and the Arts* 22 (1978): 144-66.

Schumpeter, Joseph E. *History of Economic Analysis*. New York: Oxford UP, 1954.

Shell, Marc. *Money, Language, and Thought*. Berkeley: U of California P, 1982.

Shelley, Mary. *Frankenstein, or The Modern Prometheus*. 1831. Ed. Maurice Hindle. London: Penguin, 1992.

Shinagel, Michael, ed. *Robinson Crusoe*. By Daniel Defoe. 1719. New York: W. W. Norton, 1975.

Shulman, Robert. *Social Criticism & Nineteenth-Century American Fictions*. Columbia: U of Missouri P, 1987.

Smith, Adam. *An Inquiry into the Nature and Causes of the Wealth of Nations*. Ed. R. H. Campbell and A. S. Skinner. 2 vols. Indianapolis: Liberty Classics, 1981.

———. *Lectures on Jurisprudence*. Ed. R. L Meek, D. D. Raphael, and P. G. Stein. Oxford: Clarendon Press, 1978.

———. *Lectures on Rhetoric and Belles Lettres*. Ed. J. C. Bryce. Oxford: Clarendon Press, 1983.

Smith, Johanna M. "'Cooped Up': Feminine Domesticity in *Frankenstein*." *Frankenstein: Case Studies in Contemporary Criticism*. Ed. Johanna M. Smith. Boston: St. Martin's Press, 1992. 270-85.

Starr, G. A. *Defoe and Spiritual Autobiography*. Princeton: Princeton UP, 1965.

Tompkins, Jane. *Sensational Designs: The Cultural Work of American Fiction 1790-1860*. New York: Oxford UP, 1985.

Thompson, James. *Models of Value: Eighteenth-Century Political Economy and the Novel*. Durham: Duke UP, 1996.

Trilling, Lionel. *The Liberal Imagination*. New York: Viking Press, 1950.

Trotter, David. *Circulation: Defoe, Dickens, and the Economies of the Novel*. New York: St. Martin's Press, 1988.

Veeser. Aram H., ed. *The New Historicism*. New York: Routledge, 1989.

Vernon, John. *Money and Fiction: Literary Realism in the Nineteenth and Early Twentieth Centuries*. Ithaca: Cornell UP, 1984.

Watt, Ian. *Rise of the Novel: Studies in Defoe, Richardson, and Fielding*. Berkeley: U of California P, 1967.

White, Michael. "Reading and Rewriting: The Production of an Economic Robinson Crusoe." *Southern Review: Literary and Interdisciplinary Essays* 15 (1982): 115-42.

Wolff, Richard D. and Stephen A. Resnick. *Economics: Marxian versus Neoclassical*. Baltimore: Johns Hopkins UP, 1987.

Woodmansee, Martha and Peter Jaszi, eds. *The Construction of Authorship: Textual Appropriation in Law and Literature*. Durham: Duke UP, 1994.

Zanine, Louis J. *Mechanism and Mysticism: The Influence of Science on the Thought and Work of Theodore Dreiser*. Philadelphia: U of Pennsylvania P, 1993.

Index

9780815336488

An environmentally friendly book printed and bound in England by www.printondemand-worldwide.com

PEFC Certified

This product is from sustainably managed forests and controlled sources

www.pefc.org

PEFC/16-33-415

This book is made of chain-of-custody materials; FSC materials for the cover and PEFC materials for the text pages.

#0228 - 231215 - C0 - 216/138/9 [11] - CB - 9780815336488